MORE PUB

IN

CHESHIRE AND WIRRAL

A further selection of Real Ale rambles centred on country inns with character.

Jen Darling

Alfresco Books

First published in 2000 by *Alfresco Books*
Reprinted in 2005

Mill Race, Kirkby Malham, Skipton, BD23 4BN
Tel: 01729 830868

A CIP record for this book is available from the British Library.

ISBN 1 873727 13 5

Cover - Chris Beesley

Line drawings - David Potts

Design and Typesetting - Jen Darling

Printing - Ashford Colour Press Ltd

CONTENTS

INTRODUCTION

More Pub Walks in Cheshire and Wirral is the companion volume to *Best Pub Walks in Cheshire*, published by *Sigma Leisure* in 1990. Now in a new edition, it was the first in their *Pub Walks* series and has continued to be one of their ten best sellers.

In *More Pub Walks* Jen Darling has used the ten walks which wouldn't fit into the original book and has added twenty more. She never ceases to be amazed at how rapidly the countryside changes and advises walkers to carry an up-to-date map, for example the Ordnance Survey's new *Explorer* series, in case any problems arise.

The length of each walk has been included on the Contents pages as the author thought this would be helpful. A short description of each route is also given at the start of each section.

Please, please make sure that it is alright to leave vehicles in a pub carpark before starting out, otherwise find a convenient spot nearby. The telephone numbers of featured pubs are given at the start of each walk, together with information about them.

Cheshire provides a wide variety of scenery, whether you want to enjoy windswept walks in the Pennine foothills or potter over the patchwork plain on field paths, canal towpaths, or following stretches of the long-distance routes which criss-cross the county. Included in the text is a wealth of information on local history, magical legends and the flora and fauna which enhance any trek.

I am very grateful to all those who have helped to get this manuscript ready for production. Special thanks go to: Philip Delves, who researched several of the routes; members of Lymm WI, who walked *The Peovers*; Chris Beesley, for his oil painting of the front cover; David Potts for the line drawings and Valerie West, for proof reading the final manuscript.

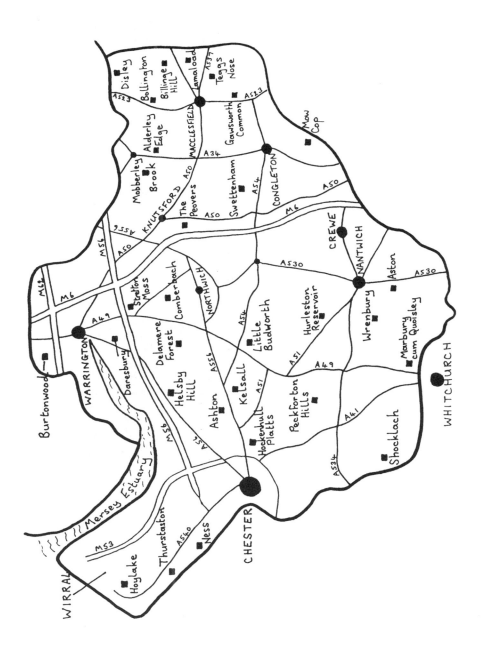

NORTH CHESHIRE

Burtonwood   *Fiddle i' th' Bag*

Explore the disused St Helen's Canal and Burtonwood village, amid flat, fertile fields of arable crops which sweep away on all sides.

Comberbach   *Spinner and Bergamot*

This field walk passes through the hamlet of Frandley with its historic Friends Meeting House.

Daresbury   *Ring o' Bells*

Visit the site of the old parsonage where Lewis Carroll was born; view the glorious memorial window in All Saints' Church. And other tributes to Daresbury's most famous son crop up all over the place, including this *Alice in Wonderland* weather vane on the village school.

Helsby Hill   *Netherton Hall*

This varied walk on sandstone paths includes one of the most spectacular views in all Cheshire!

Stretton Moss   *Stretton Fox*

Fields and mosses predominate as one explores ancient footpaths in the Manor of Stretton. (Owned by the Starkey family from the reign of Henry II until the 18th century, its emblem was a stork.)

Visible from afar is Norton's splendid water tower.

A Place to Visit

The Cycle and Cyclemotor Museum

Paul Adams opened his Cycle Museum in the Old Police Station, Runcorn, in July 1998. It was the realisation of a dream as by then he had amassed five garages full of cycling memorabilia. The museum moved to Walton Hall Gardens, south of Warrington, in 2002.

Bikes there are a-plenty — a unicycle, two-wheelers, tricycles, even a four-wheeler — and a visit here is an educational, exciting, hands-on experience. You might like to try a bone shaker, an adult tricycle or, for real adventure, a penny farthing, and, for children, there's a Triang trike, red scooters and a miniature penny farthing.

Opening times are from 10am to 4pm each weekend and Bank Holiday, with school groups and adult parties by arrangement at other times. The telephone number is 01925 601617.

Admittance is free but donations are always welcome.

AROUND BURTONWOOD

Start: Fiddle i' th' Bag (SJ 585 930)

Route: Hall Lane - St Helen's Canal - Bradlegh Old Hall - Burtonwood village - Tan House Farm - Old Alder Lane

Distance: 4.5 miles

By Car: Take the A49 from Warrington. Turn left to Burtonwood immediately opposite Winwick Church and continue along this road until the pub appears on your right.

Fiddle i' th' Bag

Tel: 01925 225442

Away to the east of the village stands the Fiddle i' th' Bag, an inn worth patronising and a convenient place to start this two-hour walk. It's the only hostelry to boast such an unusual name, which refers to a seed fiddle, once used by farmers to sow corn. One of these implements, together with the canvas bag for the corn, is preserved in the bar, and both are also depicted on the inn sign swaying in the breeze outside.

The tempting menu is displayed on several boards around the bar. All the food is home cooked and the menu changes frequently. Vegetarians are catered for and there's also a selection of *light bites* and sandwiches which, on warmer days, can be eaten outside.

The pub is open every day and serves food from 11.30am until 3pm at lunchtime and from 6 to 9pm in the evening. However, check before visiting as changes may be afoot.

Walk this way ...

Turn right as you leave the pub carpark, then immediately right again down Hall Lane. You soon pass Red House Farm which, according to records dating from 1690, used to be an important meeting place for protestant dissenters. Just past the farm buildings veer right away from the road to cross a peppermint-painted footbridge over Sankey Brook, which stands next to an old cart bridge.

This flat, rather desolate countryside (originally marsh and moss) was, not so long ago, reclaimed by 'cuts' draining into this tiny river.

Continue across the field ahead to the St Helen's Canal.

Although disused now, in 1757 this was England's first still-water canal. Its main purpose was to carry coal from St. Helens to Warrington and, by 1771, 45,000 tons was transported along it annually. How times have changed; this pleasant reach of water now provides a well-stocked haunt for Newton anglers, who silently crowd the banks hoping for catches of tench, perch, roach or bream.

Bear left along the towpath, passing a pleasant picnic spot. Then continue to a swing bridge. This one, and others along this stretch of water, were also pioneers — the first in Britain. Leave the canal here, turning left where a path takes you over Sankey Brook once more and then ascends a gentle incline. A further left turn and you are on the stony road towards Bradlegh Old Hall.

Surrounded by a moat, this is one of the oldest buildings in the area. The first hall dated from the 14th century and its worth turning aside to see the ivy encrusted gatehouse which remains from this time. The farmhouse you see today originates from the 17th century and was built using stones from the old hall.

Stories of secret passages and ghosts abound, and there are several unusual artefacts. Most notable is the oak-framed bed in the King's Room. A seven-foot-long four-poster, its measurements are roughly carved in Roman numerals and rumour has it that Cromwell slept in it and, more reliably, Richard, Duke of Gloucester, (later Richard III), on his way to repel the Scots in Lancashire.

Keep ahead until you reach the junction of Lumber Lane and Fir Tree Lane. Then plunge down the snicket opposite the bus stop, which borders a field, then continues between houses and across Phipp's Brook into Burtonwood village.

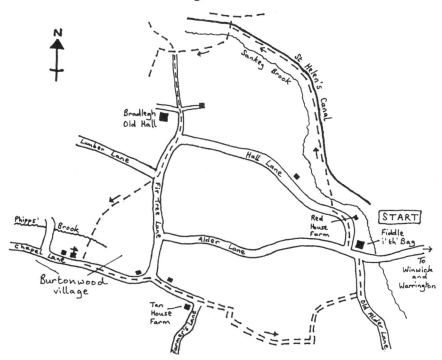

Here you may turn aside to see the church. Dating from 1716, it was extensively rebuilt in 1939 because of subsidence caused by mine workings. More recent brickwork signals more rebuilding and it is hoped that the construction of a concrete raft will finally stabilise the foundations. Inside, the building is light and airy, and each window is decked with the shield of a prominent local family: the Leghs, the Bolds and the Forshaws all have their place.

Double back along Chapel Lane, which becomes Fir Tree Lane as you round a corner. Then bear right down Farmers Lane after passing an attractive row of old, black-and-white cottages.

Ahead, the spire of Winwick Church is clearly visible, as also are the buildings of the Fiddle i'th' Bag — your journey's end.

At Tan House Farm, where the road turns sharp right, go forward along a cart-track, which turns right at a fingerpost, then swings left between flat, fertile fields.

In this somewhat bleak area Oliver Cromwell mustered his Roundhead troops in August 1648 before finally routing the Scots at Winwick. Today, agriculture abounds, staple crops of wheat, clover and hay being rotated with root crops of potatoes and turnips.

Keep bearing left at each fingerpost, enjoying far-reaching views, until, at Old Alder Lane, a final left turn takes you back to *The Fiddle*.

About Burtonwood

Although at one time the Burtonwood area was an extensive forest, by the 19th century most of the woodland had been cleared and the predominantly agricultural community provided both blacksmith and wheelwright with a healthy trade. Coal mining at nearby Collins Green has also had a considerable effect on the population.

Despite being on the northern rim of Cheshire, between the conurbations of St.Helens and Warrington, Burtonwood has (albeit precariously) retained its village identity. It is also well known for the following two developments sited on its fringe.

Founded in 1867 by James and Jane Forshaw, **Burtonwood Brewery** remained in the family for several generations, and they appear to have been generous public benefactors. They even planted the trees which still line many of the village streets today.

By 1907 the brewery was producing 200 barrels of beer a week and today the Company owns about 300 pubs in Lancashire, Cheshire, Staffordshire and North Wales. A new brewhouse was opened in September 1990, and a painting of the brewery by Gordon Firth, a local artist, was presented to each member of the workforce.

During the 2nd World War **Burtonwood Airforce Base** became the largest military establishment outside the USA. The area was selected as an ideal site for an airfield as it comprised flat land with good drainage, was close to towns and industry, and next to a railway line.

American soldiers soon arrived at the base and the church's marriage registers indicate how attractive these young GI's were to the local girls! Visiting celebrities during the war years included Bing Crosby, Bob Hope and James Cagney. However, although aircraft were serviced there for the Berlin Airlift, after the war use of the base gradually dwindled and the M62 now traverses the main runway.

AROUND COMBERBACH

Start: The Spinner and Bergamot (SJ 647 775)

Route: Gibb Hill - Deakin Yard - Frandley - Sandiway Lane - Senna Lane - Cogshall Brook - Comberbach

Distance: 5 miles

By Car: From Warrington, take the A49 south to the M56 roundabout. Continue south on the A559 for 3 miles, then turn right into Comberbach down Gibb Hill. The *Spinner*'s carpark is on the right after Bergamot Lane.

The Spinner & Bergamot

Tel: 01606 891307

The word *bergamot* has three meanings: an old English herb, a sweet orange (the rind of which produces the fragrant oil, essence of bergamot) and a luscious type of pear. The pub's name, however, was derived from two successful racehorses, owned by James Smith Barry of nearby Marbury Hall in the 18th century.

Today, *The Spinner* is still a traditional, homely village inn, with log fires in Winter and no children or music. Toby jugs adorn the oak beams, together with horse brasses. These, inherited from a family in Moore (a village near Runcorn) show sets of crowns and suits of cards. The dining room is non-smoking.

Food is served every lunchtime, from noon to 2pm (3pm on Sunday) and every evening except Monday. The menu is supplemented by a 'specials' board and all the food is home-made. There's always a casserole, a curry, a chilli or stroganoff, and a choice for vegetarians.

Real Ale includes Greenalls' cask bitter and two guest beers — maybe Marston's *Pedigree*, Flowers' *Original* or Timothy Taylor's *Landlord*. Recently, *The Spinner* has won a *Pub of the Year* and a *Best Kept Kitchen* award. Walkers with muddy boots are welcome on the tiled floor of the left-hand bar. Non-muddy boots are welcome anywhere!

Walk this way ...

Turn left and walk back up Gibb Hill to the A559.

A gibbet once stood here and was used for executions — hence the name. It was succeeded by a small garage and a smithy.

Turn right and immediately left down Pole Lane. Here, North Lodge guards the drive to Belmont Hall and the milestone dates from 1896.

Pass the entrance to *The Pole*, then turn left down the track in front of Pole Farm Cottage. Pass a house on the left and bear right into the field at a row of wooden barns. Turn left behind these to a gateway.

The Pole is named after an ancient family called de la Pole. At one time the estate belonged to the Eaton family — large Cheshire landowners from the 17th to the 20th century.

The tractor track over the next field takes you behind a pond. Continue with the hedge on your left, turn right into the next field along a short cart-track, then bear left beside the hedge. Exit by a smallish gate and turn right along a muddy track, which continues alongside the wood known as Deakin Yard.

Deakin Yard is thought to have been named after a man buried here. It is documented as having been a fox covert and a plantation, and today contains oak, ash, sycamore and holly.

Exit by the gate and continue on a grassy track. At the end of the next field bear left over a stile, then keep the hedge on your right to exit over a corner stile. Turn left, then right along the A559 for a short distance, before turning right over a stile opposite Frandley House.

*Originally a small farm, **Frandley House** became the home of Major A W Boyd from 1919 until his death in 1959. He was a naturalist, bird watcher and well known authority on rural customs and dialect.*

After the death of T A Coward, he took over the weekly articles on the countryside printed in the Manchester Guardian for many years. He also wrote two books — A Country Parish and The Diary of a Country Man — and published the soulcakers' play still performed by the Comberbach Mummers. Spoken of as 'a lovely couple', he and his wife, Violet, are buried nearby at St Mark's Church, Antrobus.

Cross the huge field facing you, aiming for Fox Farm (the building to the right of a row of semi-detached houses.)

Once an inn, then two cottages, now a private house, Fox Farm also boasts a particularly attractive, renovated barn.

Climb over the stile here. Turn left back along the A559, then immediately right towards the Friends Meeting House and Frandley — a small hamlet on the hill's brow.

On the corner as you turn right stands Frandley Farm. Dating from about 1790, the present farmhouse is a prime example of Georgian architecture. Built of bricks made from local clay, it has an imposing entrance and huge chimneys flush with the gable ends. Placed symmetrically, the windows have stone sills and wedge lintels anchored by a keystone. These houses were a sign of wealth when farm labourers still existed in 'cruck' cottages with no sanitation.

Turn left down Sandiway Lane at the next junction, towards Comberbach and Little Leigh.

On your right here stands Frandley Brow House. Covered in virginia creeper, it has had a varied history, having been a school, a brewery, a joiner's workshop and, finally, a busy and successful village store with a seven-day licence to sell liquor. Sadly, it closed in 1971.

You soon pass the Friends Meeting House — a haven of peace.

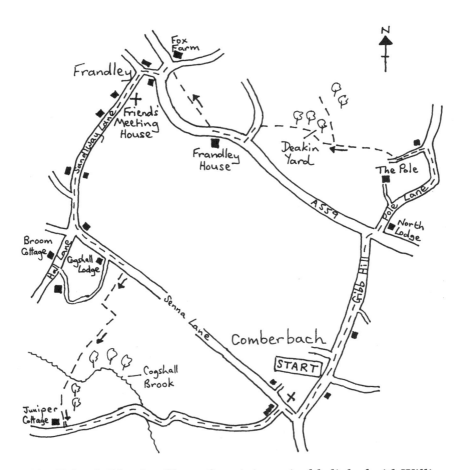

The Friends Meeting House *here is inextricably linked with William Gandy, one-time owner of Frandley Farm, who became a Quaker. His friend, George Fox, founder of the Movement, visited several times, preaching to over 3,000 people in the open air and in 1676 William Gandy gave a building on the plot of land here, to be used as a meeting house. Today's building, however, dates from 1881 and its high windows prevent any outside distraction for worshippers!*

The women's meeting room next door dates from the 17th century, when women were not allowed into the men's meetings. Today, the lower floor, once stabling, has been converted into kitchens, and the meeting room above is used for social functions.

Once well-to-do farmers, the Gandys were so persecuted for their religious beliefs, fined for non-attendance at Great Budworth Church and for holding outdoor meetings (dubbed 'riotous gatherings') that they were left virtually penniless and emigrated to North America.

The name 'Quaker' is thought to originate either from when George Fox was arrested and told a judge that he too should quake before the name of the Lord, or that a Friend feeling called to speak at a meeting will often quake (tremble) at the prospect.

Known as Seven Oaks, this area is thought to have been named after seven oak trees which once grew here. The last one blew down in 1970 but its stump can still be seen in the corner of the grounds of the Friends Meeting House where, in 1897, seven new oaks were planted to commemorate Queen Victoria's Diamond Jubilee.

From the hilltop, panoramic views stretch across the Cheshire plain to Beeston Castle and you soon pass several farmsteads.

***Frandley Brow Farm** is the only working farm in Frandley. Dairy farming was the principal agriculture in Cheshire for centuries and this farm still has its dairy herd. It also produces crops of wheat, barley and potatoes.*

***Sandiway Farm** is another example of Georgian architecture.*

Ignore the right turn down Scotch Hall Lane and keep straight on at the crossroads, where Senna Green Farm has some fine buildings and produces pig and poultry meat.

*Down Hall Lane you can just see white-coated **Broom Cottage**, thought to be the oldest dwelling in the area. Built as a two-up, two-down 'cruck' cottage, its character has been faithfully preserved, together with the original, old oak beams.*

You soon pass Cogshall Lodge, which has guarded this entrance to Cogshall Hall since 1830. Peter Jackson, the hall's owner at that time, wished to build a church here to serve the estate and the villages of Antrobus and Comberbach. Although permission was refused by the Bishop of Chester, the crucifix shape of the lodge is symbolic.

Turn right along a footpath in front of the ANTROBUS village sign. Walk down beside the hedge through a spinney of bramble and oak, then holly, sycamore and elder, to a rhododendron patch. Turn left at its end to continue through beech and hawthorn, then exit over a stile.

Keep ahead across the field, on slightly raised, rough ground with a hedge over to your left. Climb into the next field over a piece of fence between barbed wire, bear left over a stile then right down the side of the field to another.

Keep in the same direction through a pretty copse, enhanced by snowberry and hawthorn. The grassy bank near Cogshall Brook makes an idyllic picnic spot before you cross the stream between beech and ash, then climb over a stile.

Nearby, the brook cascades noisily over a mini-waterfall and a dry-stonewall signifies the edge of the Cogshall estate.

Keep ahead, aiming for Juniper Cottage. Cross the rubberised section of electric fence on your left, walk through the gate, then down the short drive to the road. Turn left to cross Cogshall Brook again and wind up the hill past farms to right and left. As you enter Comberbach rows of terraced cottages lead up to the imposing Wesleyan chapel.

Erected in 1879, to the same design as Frandley's Friends Meeting House, this imposing building, with its ornate plasterwork, was once also used as a school.

Turn right along Senna Lane, then left up Warrington Road, passing the imposing Mulberry House and grounds, followed by Brookfield Road, to arrive back at *The Spinner.*

AROUND DARESBURY

Start: Ring o' Bells (SJ 579 829)

Route: Old Chester Road - Newton Lane - Summer Lane - Morphany Lane (Lewis Carroll's birthplace) - Black Jane Farm - Queasty Birch Hall - Hatton - Row's Wood - Hobb Lane (Moore) - Bridgewater Canal - Keckwick Lane - All Saints Church

Distance: 8 miles

By Car: Take the A56 south from Warrington. Take the next left turn after the A558 to Runcorn. Turn right immediately into the Ring o' Bells carpark.

Ring o' Bells
Tel: 01925 740256

Only a field separates the inn from the church and the original inn sign showed the bells being rung. Dating from early in the 19th century, the Ring o' Bells was originally a farm, which became the village *local* when the farmer decided to brew his own beer. Eventually he was granted a licence and a Mr Davenport was the last man to be both farmer and publican. Another licensee, named Hewitt, was a huntsman with the Cheshire hounds.

The adjoining Sessions Room (now part of the pub) was the courthouse where Daresbury Petty Sessions were held once a month until they moved to Stockton Heath in 1911. Later, the Lewis Carroll Society leased the building from local brewers, *Greenall Whitley*, for a nominal rent of 10s 6d — the price tag on the Mad Hatter's hat!

The adjacent parish room was originally a sandstone barn but is now a village amenity. The old stables, adjacent to the pub's carpark, used to house the parish hearse and its use was free to local people. Later, the wide doorway, necessary to accommodate it, was blocked up.

The pub itself was a coaching inn for many years. The coach arrived at noon on its way from Warrington to Chester and The Square nearby provided enough space for the horses to be turned. The mounting block for riders can still be found behind the wall.

Nowadays, the *Ring o' Bells* is still very traditional, both in design and decor, and is well used by village 'regulars' and visitors. It is open all day every day. Food is served at lunchtime and in the evening during the week but snacks are available all day on Saturday and food is served all day on Sunday. The varied chalkboard menu is changed daily and includes many vegetarian dishes. For warmer days, the outside seating area extends across the large, landscaped garden.

Walk this way ...

Turn right up the village street (Chester Old Road).

Daresbury village is full of old world charm, its church and inn, pretty cottages and farm buildings all blending harmoniously together. Look out for the Cheshire cat grinning out from the eaves of a barn on your left. Well Cottage was so named because the village pump stood in its garden and the post office is now a private house.

Dating from 1600, the village school must be one of the oldest still in use in Cheshire. The Alice in Wonderland weather vane was made by the local blacksmith and originally stood on the roof of the village smithy (now Duttons).

At the end of the village turn left through a kissing gate and follow the slight line of a path diagonally across this huge field to another kissing gate. Drop straight down the next field, then keep ahead beside the wood to Newton Lane.

Go ahead towards Newton Bank Farm, then turn right down a bridleway which goes under the M56. From here, continue forward up to Little Manor Farm, walk through the farmyard and down the farm road to Summer Lane.

Enjoy extensive views of the Overton Hills as you turn left here and, after passing a row of cottages on the hilltop, turn right down the track to Hallam Hall Farm. At a bend keep ahead over a stile and continue in the same direction beside the hedgerow all the way down to Morphany Lane. Turn right to reach Lewis Carroll's birthplace.

***Charles Lutwidge Dodgson** (better known as Lewis Carroll) was born here in January 1832, when his father was Vicar of All Saints' Church, Daresbury. And it was here that the young Charles spent the first eleven years of his life.*

Until recently, the site was marked simply by a roadside plinth, inscribed with a quote from Lewis Carroll's poem, Three Sunsets, in which he refers to this very spot:
> *An island farm, midst seas of corn,*
> *Swayed by the wandering breath of morn,*
> *The happy spot where I was born ...*

The plinth remains but, since the site of the old parsonage (burnt down in 1883) was excavated in June 1990, there is more to see, including the ground plan of the building, and the well.

Continue to Higher Lane and turn left. (Notice Glebe Farm. Was it once church property?) Then take the next left turn up Newton Lane.

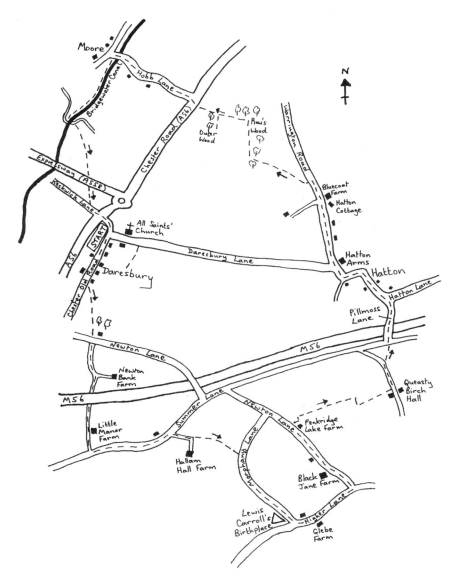

Dating from 1729, the farmhouse of Black Jane Farm is a superb Georgian building of symmetrical design, with solid stone quoins, lintels and window-sills. Notice too the weather vane depicting Alice and a Cheshire cat. Black Jane herself is reputed to have been a swarthy-complexioned farmer's wife who brewed a very potable ale!

Continue until you turn right down the drive of Penkridge Lake Farm, bear left at the farmhouse, then right between barns to a stile. From here, keep ahead along the fence to a corner stile, then make for the oak near the far side of the facing field and the stile in the hedge behind it. Cross the bridge here and continue forward on a tractor track, until you turn right down the facing hedge to a stile in it.

Keep ahead again, beside the hedge, then climb the stile into the farmyard of Queasty Birch Hall. Continue forward through gates and between barns, then cross the farm track to a stile in the palisade. Walk behind the farmhouse, negotiate two more stiles and turn left along the farm road — cobbled at first.

Where the road bends left keep ahead over a stile, then down the field's side and up a flight of mossy steps. Cross Summer Lane and the motorway (on Pillmoss Lane), before veering left down Hatton Lane (B5356).

From here you have a good view of the sandstone water tower at Norton. Built in 1890 to supply Liverpool with water from Lake Vyrnwy in North Wales, it's been a dominant local landmark ever since.

You soon pass the Hatton Arms, which may be open! The home-made soup, salads and sandwiches are highly recommended.

Stay on this road, ignoring all footpaths until you have passed Hatton Cottage and Bluecoat Farm, then turn left through a wooden kissing gate, waymarked to Moore, two miles. Walk ahead to another gate (behind a hedge), then stay almost parallel with the stream, which gushes from an underground pipe here, to reach another kissing gate.

From here, veer left and walk alongside a ditch to a kissing gate at the entrance to Row's Wood. Continue through this pretty bluebell wood, crossing the stream and exiting at the far side. Then turn right to follow the field's edge and the wood, underplanted with bamboo, all the way round to a gate. Here, go through a facing kissing gate, waymarked to Chester Road.

Walk up the field, following the fence then veering left on a narrow path to the corner of Outer Wood. Turn right beside this and drop down to Chester Road. Cross with care and walk down Hobb Lane, its sturdy sandstone walls topped by banks of daffodils in Spring.

Look out for the clear-cut, concrete cylinder, outstanding landmark for miles around, which dwarfs the other buildings and landscaped lawns of Daresbury Laboratory, opened by Prime Minister, Harold Wilson, in 1967.

Cross the Bridgewater Canal and turn left along the towpath.

*The reeds on the opposite bank provide shelter for swans, mallards, moorhens and coots, and you have views of Runcorn Bridge and Fiddler's Ferry Power Station. Engineering feat of James Brindley in the 18th century, the remarkably straight course of the **Bridgewater Canal** revolutionised coal transport from Manchester to the sea.*

Leave the canal at the next bridge, walking over it and bearing right through a gate. Then cross straight over the field, on a path between crops, to a stile. Veer diagonally right over the next field, then turn right along its far side and drop down to a stream. Follow the path across a rough area to steps behind a blackthorn.

Cross the expressway (A558) with care and drop down steps between hawthorn, gorse and blackthorn, then take the path diagonally left up the field and turn left up Keckwick Lane. Cross the busy A56 and continue forward down Old Chester Road back to the Ring o' Bells.

All Saints' Church, Daresbury

With its many Lewis Carroll connections, the church itself is well worth a visit and is open on weekend afternoons from 2 to 4.30 pm. Anyone requiring more information should ring either Irene Rutter on 01928 713815 or the Vicar on 01925 740348.

Daresbury is famous worldwide for its Lewis Carroll connections. Born Charles Lutwidge Dodgson, his father was Vicar here throughout much of his childhood, although the family lived at the former parsonage on Morphany Lane, two miles away. Outside, by the main entrance, is the 16th century font in which the baby, Charles, was baptised by his father, who would also have preached each Sunday from the Jacobean pulpit, with its exquisite carvings of angels, grotesques, and a gryphon — featured in Carroll's work.

The splendid memorial window in a side chapel depicts Lewis Carroll with Alice and several of the animals in his famous stories — the Mad Hatter, White Rabbit and the Dormouse in its teapot. It's a treat too to listen to a detailed description of each feature incorporated into the richly stained glass, and mementoes are for sale.

The tower is the oldest part of the church and dates from the 16th century. It houses a ground floor ring of eight bells, and an unusual rhyme in the ringing chamber is written as an acrostic, the initial letters of each line spelling out the word, DARESBURY. When the bells are not ringing, the mellow Westminster chimes of the church clock ring out loud and clear each quarter hour.

Other notable features are the unique green man carved into the 16th century panelling behind the altar, which originally formed a rood screen separating choir and congregation. And, in the south aisle, notice the saints depicted in the colourful windows, particularly Saint Bartholomew, who was skinned alive and is actually carrying his skin like a stole — an arm complete with hand. Yuck!

AROUND HELSBY HILL

Start: Netherton Hall (SJ 512 770)

Route: Carriage Drive - Dunsdale - Beacon Hill - Shepherds'
Houses - Snidley Moor - The Ridgeway - Hill Road North
- Helsby Hill - Old Chester Road - Bates Lane - The Holt

Distance: 6.5 miles

By Car: Take the A56 east from Chester. Continue through Helsby
village. *Netherton Hall* is then on the left half-a-mile
before Frodsham.

Netherton Hall

Tel: 01928 732342

The original building on this site was a manor house in which,
according to old deeds, Robert de Netherton resided in 1325, followed
by William in 1390. In the reign of Henry VIII the family of
Nangreaves lived here and had an estate nearby at Woodhouses. The
building on the site at that time is documented as being 'an old stone
mansion in the style of James I's reign, standing on a knoll half-a-mile
from Frodsham'. The Nangreaves died out in 1815.

The hall was then demolished and replaced by a farm, worked first by Ralph Bate from 1865 to 1902, then by Arthur Clarke for 45 years. His son, Sydney, then took over, but died aged only 35. (Sydney's sister Eileen, and her son, John, were both born in the farmhouse.)

An old toll board on the wall dates from 1812, when the A56 was a toll road from Chester and charges were made at Trafford Gate and Netherton Gate. It cost 6d to pass through the first gate and 3d the second, but pricing also varied according to a vehicle's width.

The hall was converted into a pub in 1982 — the newest one in Frodsham. Nearby, a pile of grassy rubble is all that is left of *The Whalebone* — the original Netherton 'local'.

Today, the rooms retain some of the hall's ambience with their names — the library, lounge, study and parlour. (And the loos are named Squires and Maids.) There's supposed to be a gentleman ghost too called *Old Charlie*. Seen standing at the bar by Sheila, the cleaning lady who's worked here since 1985, he disappeared into thin air when she turned to serve him.

Netherton Hall is open seven days a week, from noon onwards, and food is served each lunchtime and evening. Bar snacks are available all day at the weekend, and during the week if there's a chef about. Chicken and leek croissant, Danish rollmop herrings and home-made vegetable paté are three of the appetising snacks on offer.

All the food is freshly cooked and home-made and (how refreshing) there's rosti instead of chips! The blackboard menu caters for both traditional and adventurous palates, and ostrich is sometimes on offer. The hall has also built up a reputation for its traditional Sunday lunch, with a choice of roast beef and another joint.

Five different Real Ales are served, which change regularly. (Jennings is a popular choice.) The wine list is extensive. Six whites and six reds from various countries — France, Germany, Spain, Chile and the Antipodes — can be bought by glass or bottle.

Walk this way ...

Cross the A56 with care and walk ahead up Carriage Drive. Continue uphill in the same direction until you reach the Jack Baker Memorial, put up in 1981 at the junction of tracks in Dunsdale.

Jack Baker was a well known Frodsham walker, and the originator of both the Sandstone Trail and the lesser known Baker Way — a route of 10 miles from Chester to Delamere Forest.

From here, the adventurous can climb the red, sandstone cliffs known as Jacob's Ladder on the left, while the more sedate can ascend via steps ahead. Keep on the path alongside the golf course for a short distance, then turn right through the gorse to walk straight across it, towards Beacon Hill. A short footpath then takes you onto Simons Lane. Turn left to pass the Beacon Hill car park and the start of the Sandstone Trail.

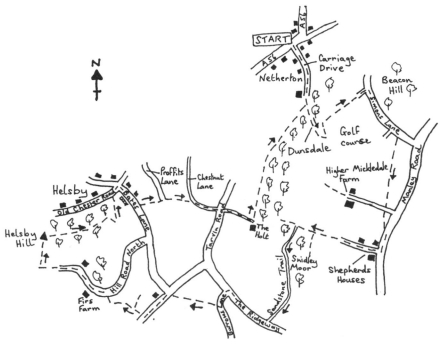

32 miles long, the Sandstone Trail follows the ridge down the length of the county, from Frodsham to Grindley Brook, near Whitchurch.

After the entrance to Frodsham Golf Course turn right through a hedge gap and walk ahead beside the golfers' practice area. Continue between hawthorn hedge and leylandii to the farm road to Higher Mickledale. Cross this and the next field, veering slightly left to a stile onto Manley Road.

Turn right to Shepherds' Houses, where you turn right again down a farm track. Keep ahead through a gate onto a footpath. Ignore the left turn to Snidley Moor and go down wide, sandy steps to a rough-hewn bench, dedicated by the Woodland Trust to Irene Kathleen Miles.

Turn left here along the Sandstone Trail and follow it to the road known as The Ridgeway. Turn right downhill. (On high is the Foxhill lookout tower.) Take the first left turn along Burrows Lane, aptly named as rabbits abound. Then bear right through a kissing gate. (You are now on the Longster Trail.)

Ten miles long, the Longster Trail runs from Piper's Ash, on the outskirts of Chester, to the top of Helsby Hill. It was devised by Frank Longster of Frodsham for the Mid-Cheshire Footpath Society, the members of which waymark and maintain the route.

Walk along the field's side with a stream on your right. At a barbed wire fence, turn right to cross the stream and go through a steel kissing gate, before continuing in the same direction to the road.

Turn left, passing Teuthill House and climbing the hill before turning right along a track signposted Hill Road and Helsby Hill. This soon becomes a footpath, which you follow to a stile ahead. After this turn right up the bank, veer left round the side of the field and exit over another stile. In the next field you soon turn right through a kissing gate, then walk along a hedge to a steel gate and Hill Road North.

Turn left uphill to Harmers Lake Farm, passing Firs Farm on the way. Veer left along a track, signposted Alvanley Road. At the next sign turn right onto National Trust property and walk up to the summit of Helsby Hill.

What a view! Landmarks stand out two-a-penny, from the cathedrals and docks of Liverpool to the elegant, single span of Runcorn Bridge. And, on a clear day, the plain rolls away to the Cumbrian fells in the north and the unbroken ridges of the Pennine chain in the east. Don't forget to look behind at Beeston Castle too .

Then, almost beneath your feet, is the site of an Iron Age fort. Established as early as 100BC on a perfect vantage point from which to repel any attack, today it forms an idyllic picnic spot.

Helsby Hill, with its distinctive, sphinx-like features, forms a prominent landmark above the Mersey valley.

From the trig point (464 feet above sea level) turn right past a clump of gorse and descend the hill on a path between stunted oak, which can be muddy. Keep right after going down steps and meeting a main track, then go right again for a short distance and leave the National Trust land over a stile. Turn left here down a gorse-filled valley, eventually slipping through a snicket to Old Chester Road.

The name, Helsby, is derived from an old Norse word meaning 'village on the ledge', but this road is of Roman origin. Built on the ledge of higher ground right under the crag itself, it joined Deva (Chester) with Roman settlements at Wilderspool, near Warrington, and Mamucium (Manchester). A Roman camp defended the highway and, in 1958, a Roman altar was discovered nearby.

Turn right, then right again up Bates Lane. After the sandstone terrace of quarrymen's cottages (for this was a thriving local industry in the 19th century) turn left through a gate onto a footpath. Climb over a stile and cross a field, veering left to a stile, a plank bridge and the end of Proffits Lane.

Go down a snicket, between hedges of beech and privet, to a stream. Continue across a field and turn right up Chestnut Lane at the ford. Turn left along Tarvin Road, then immediately right to *The Holt*. On reaching this, turn left before a white gate and go through a kissing gate. Take the footpath along the wood's edge, signposted to Frodsham, all the way to a superbly-built sandstone wall.

Climb uphill beside this to reach your first footpath again. Turn left along it, retracing your steps back to Netherton Hall.

AROUND STRETTON MOSS

Start: Stretton Fox (SJ 622 823)

Route: *Ring o'Bells* - Walnut Tree Farm - School Lane - Bentley's Farm Lane - *Birch & Bottle* - Fogg's Farm - Antrobus Golf Course - Whitley Reed Farm - Appleton Moss - Stretton Moss - Moss Hall Lane - Summit Close

Distance: 6 miles

By Car: From Warrington, take the A49 south to the M56 roundabout. Take the first left turn off this to the *Stretton Fox* carpark.

Stretton Fox

Tel: 01925 732991

The history of the building dates back to the 19th century, when Liverpool was one of the country's leading ports, handling thousands of cattle which arrived regularly from Canada and the Argentine. At that time dairy farming predominated in the area, with fresh milk, eggs and vegetables sent to London for sale.

To service this growing industry, a number of farmhouses sprang up in the middle of the 1800s, one of which was Spark Hall — now the *Stretton Fox*. It is believed to have been built by Peter Leather, who

moved in with his wife, Winifred, a Robert Leather and a Mr Robertson. This family remained at the house until around 1920 when it was sold to the Blackshaw family.

The land on which the farmhouse was built is recorded on the 1840 tithe map as *Spark Field* and, at that time, it belonged to Nathaniel Dennis Miller, a wealthy local landowner. The unusual name of *Spark* is thought to have been derived from a small fish of the trout family, known as a *spark* or a *spa*, which was to be found in both a small pond in front of the house and a larger one across the road.

The *Stretton Fox* stands beside the site of the Roman road which ran from Wilderspool to Northwich, then on to London, and the name of *Stretton* (the town on the street) dates from this time.

Today the *Stretton Fox* is a thriving inn, well used by both locals and businessmen. It is open for food and drink seven days a week, from noon until 9.30pm (9pm on Sundays). Its menu is changed quarterly, according to the season. Vegetarians are well catered for and there are 'specials' boards. The majority of the pub is smoke-free.

Hancocks Best Bitter is a popular Real Ale and London Pride is often available in Winter, when you might also be able to enjoy a hot toddy by one of the three real fires. In Summer jugs of Pimms are popular.

Walkers are always welcome, whether a single soul or a crowd. (It is, however, appreciated if the leader says they are parking, then patronising the pub afterwards.)

Walk this way ...

Return to the roundabout and turn left over the motorway. Take the next left turn down the A559 towards Northwich and you soon pass the *Ring o' Bells*.

This unspoilt village 'local' specialises in good beer and the unusual inn sign is a portrait of the late Tom Galley, a bell ringer at the nearby

St Matthew's Church, Stretton, for more than 60 years, and a well known local character.

Take care along this busy road with its narrow pavement and, after passing Stretton House, dated 1769-88, and a pond, turn right over a stile in the hedge. Go ahead across the field, making for the corner of the farm buildings. Walk alongside these and turn left onto a cart-track at the far end. Almost immediately turn right over a stile in the hedge and cut the corner off this field as you make for another stile.

Cross the next field (perhaps a messy mire at first) aiming for the kink in the hedge opposite. Negotiate the stile here and bear right beside the hedge to another stile, after which you turn left along School Lane.

Ignore the right turn into Booth's Lane, then turn right over a stile, and negotiate nettles, just before the outbuildings of Noggin Cottage. Bear left along the hedge here, rounding the bend in it to a pond and stile in the field's corner.

Keep a look out for heron as the numerous ponds provide fertile fishing grounds.

Turn right along the hedge of the next field. Climb over the stile into the following field and turn left along the hedge to a stile and road junction at Bentley's Farm.

(The friendly farmer here not only provided bales of hay for use as outside seating at my son's wedding reception in the local village hall, but was also kind enough to arrange them in a horseshoe shape.)

Turn left along Bentley's Farm Lane to the *Birch & Bottle*. Cross the A559 and continue down Birch Tree Lane, passing some 18th century property on the way to Fogg's Farm. Keep ahead at the junction here, first between farm buildings and a modern bungalow, then past fishing pools to Antrobus Golf Course.

The management are to be commended as great care has been taken to point walkers in the right direction.

Walk beside the course, passing more ponds, then continue on a gravel path until it bears right after the last pond and peters out. From here make for a post ahead and turn left along a rough, and perhaps muddy, cart-track.

Veer right at the next post and cross the course, with care, to a facing marker at the end of a ditch. Turn left here, continuing between young trees past another post, then leave the course via a stile in the right-hand corner of the facing hedge.

Turn right along the top edge of two fields, then turn left along Reed Lane. Keep ahead at the sharp bend, down a rough road known locally as New Occupation Lane, which leads to Whitley Reed Farm.

Barns, built here in 1940 by the War Agricultural Committee, have today been turned into private dwellings. You are about to cross part of Whitley Reed, which provided peat for fuel in Roman times. Still somewhat wild and wet, 15th century records state that the Reed was strictly controlled for pasturing animals (mainly cattle) and taking turves for fuel. Much of the wasteland has now been drained and cleared for the cultivation of grass for silage and potatoes. However, there are still rough patches where gorse, heather, reeds, brambles and sweet gale flourish.

As you reach the farm turn left and walk through a rough patch of nettles. Then take the same direction through rough grass alongside a hedge, a fence, then on a slight ridge which separates fields.

The woodland ahead was once a part of Stretton Moss. Look out for marlpits too, which can still be seen in many Cheshire fields. In the 19th century marl was dug from fertile areas around the mosses and spread as fertiliser over the fields. The shallow bank on one side, where the cart would be backed up for loading, today enables cattle to drink easily.

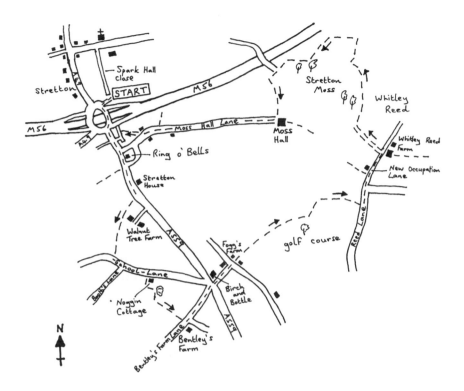

At the deep ditch ahead turn right and walk to a wooden bridge and a stile into the next field. Keep ahead, with the fence on your left, to another stile. After this cross a small area of rough ground, then a sandy racetrack, to reach the end of a hedge. Continue ahead to the left of this until you veer left past ponds teeming with wildlife, cross the sandy track again and make for the stile ahead.

If crops allow, bear slightly left to the motorway and turn left beside it. At the field's end bear left again, following the hedge up to the wood. Veer slightly right and follow its edge, then continue on the rough patch of grass separating crops to reach a gravel track.

Turn left here, away from the motorway and, after a short distance where it bears left, leave it and veer right up the side of a field towards Moss Hall. Keep ahead at the first stile, then turn right over the second to walk beside the slurry pit. Next, bear left alongside the byre until you cross the stile next to a field gate.

Turn right along Moss Hall Lane where, in Autumn, an abundance of blackberries are there for the picking. Just past the buildings of Tanyard Farm turn right over an almost hidden stile by a white gate. From here cross the field, keeping the telegraph pole on your right and eventually walking alongside a jutting-out hedge to a corner stile.

Turn left, then right along Summit Close to reach the A559. Turn right to cross the motorway, then back down Spark Hall Close to the *Stretton Fox*.

*Ahead is **St Matthew's Church**, Stretton, built in 1827 and restored in 1870. On a clear day seven counties can be seen from the top of its tower, which has six bells and a clock with two faces, on which the words, 'Time is not all' and 'Forget not God', replace the numerals.*

MID-CHESHIRE

Ashton   *Golden Lion*

A lovely walk this, on a breezy, bright day, with Ashton church spire pointedly positioned above the plain, and the charming village nestling below in the midst of farming country.

Delamere Forest   *Tiger's Head*

Delamere Forest abounds with history, from Iron Age forts to the Forestry Commission's land use. Many people visit the forest annually for a range of activities: walking, cycling, orienteering, watching wildlife — and there's even a wheelchair trail.

Kelsall   *The Boot in Boothsdale*

Following part of the Sandstone Trail, this walk, from one of Cheshire's most attractive pubs, provides breathtaking views, plus snippets of history and folklore along the way.

Little Budworth   *Red Lion*

Enjoy placid pools and silver birch trees' dappled shade on Little Budworth Common, then a peaceful glimpse of Oulton Park — one of England's premier motor racing circuits.

Peckforton Hills   *Pheasant Inn*

I make no apology for including another walk from one of my favourite Cheshire inns, which also features on the cover of *Best Pub Walks in Cheshire*. The route also takes in Beeston Castle and explores some of the county's most attractive scenery.

Places to Visit

Blakemere Craft Centre
The land at Blakemere was originally owned by Lord Barrymore of nearby Marbury. Sadly, Blakemere Hall was demolished in 1950, but the stable block, dating from 1890, has had a varied history, having been used for the manufacture of Jones sewing machines, as kennels for greyhounds, then as a bakery during the 2nd World War.

Today's crafts include flowers and furniture, teddy bears and tableware, chocolates, cards, clocks and clothing. There's also a children's play barn, aquatic goods, falconry and a restaurant. (Tel: 01606 883261)

Cheshire Herbs
.. is a nursery, on the A49 near Little Budworth, selling a large range of culinary and medicinal plants. Here, you can wander around the herb garden, obtain expert information and browse in the delightful giftshop. (Tel: 01829 760578)

Beeston Market and Chas. Hardern's Canal Shop
Beeston market, which takes place every Wednesday, is known as the *Smithfield of the North*. Visit it, then climb the wooden outdoor staircase to enter Chas. Hardern's canal shop — a real Aladdin's cave.

The Candle Factory at Burwardsley (now Cheshire Workshops)
This started as a tiny cottage industry in White Cottage (now demolished) further down the hill, when a father and daughter demonstrated the making of sand candles to pupils visiting Burwardsley's Outdoor Education Centre. The children bought the candles and gradually the business grew, eventually moving to the barns of Willow Hill Farm, where it is now.

Today, candle making is but part of this thriving concern. Many country products can be purchased and food is served in the restaurant. (Tel: 01829 770401)

AROUND ASHTON

Start: The Golden Lion (SJ 505 692)

Route: Ashton Lane - Peel Hall - Ashton Church - West End

Distance: 2 to 3 miles

By Car: Travelling east from Chester along the A54, turn left to Ashton off the Tarvin and Kelsall by-pass. *The Golden Lion* faces you and there's a large carpark behind.

The Golden Lion
Tel: 01829 751508

The building, which is over 300 years old, was originally a farm and the conversion to country inn included both farmhouse and barn. Today you can slake your thirst with a range of cask ales and there's a different guest beer every week.

Food is served every lunchtime and evening, and all day at the weekend. The home-made food always includes a soup-of-the-day, and ostrich or kangaroo are two of the unusual 'specials' sometimes on offer. Vegetarians have plenty of choice and walking groups can order from the menu before their walk.

Walk this way ...

The Golden Lion is the starting point and, as you set off, notice the bricked-up doorway of the cottage opposite — once the entrance to the village shop. Then walk back along Ashton Lane past the Methodist Chapel, built in 1888, and turn right over a stile.

From here you can see the tower of Ashton's mother church at Tarvin, as it stands four-square above the plain.

Go ahead down the side of the field to cross a further stile and turn left down a rutted track where, in early Spring, celandines wave shining, daisylike heads, sheltered by banks topped with hawthorn. Beeston Castle and the Peckforton Hills are clearly outlined above the plain and the Welsh hills form a misty, distant backdrop.

At the track's end cross a stile, then turn left and continue round two sides of this field to reach steps down to a stout plank over the stream — tributary of Salters Brook. Take care as you cross, then turn right alongside it. At the field's end climb over a stile and turn left.

The gaunt, grey mass of Peel Hall looms suddenly ahead — grim reminder of the area's troubled history, first against the Welsh, then later in Royalist times. This building replaced a much older motte and bailey and, in 1690, William III stayed here with a large party on his way to Hoylake, to sail for Ireland and the Battle of the Boyne. Inside is a magnificent oak staircase, down which guests once made a swirling exit from the ballroom for a scrumptious supper served in the kitchen below.

Little remains of the moat which originally surrounded the house and was the source of a local ghost story, which tells of a young daughter of the family who stole out each evening to meet her illicit lover. Arriving home one fateful night to find the drawbridge raised, in a panic she set her horse to jump the wide moat. The blood-curdling shrieks that may still be heard at night, echoing over the surrounding countryside, are said to be the frantic screams as both horse and mistress drowned in the ice-cold, black water.

To return to the present day, in the far distance the industrial landscape spreads along the southern banks of the Mersey, the cooling towers of Ince power station prominent on the skyline.

Climb over a stile by a gate and continue in the same direction, then veer left to a stile before farm buildings. Turn right here and continue past Peel Hall and along its drive as it sweeps right. When you reach

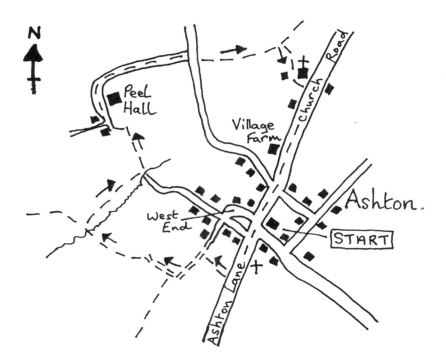

a country lane cross it, then negotiate two stiles to walk along the hedge under a sandy hill, where rabbits aplenty scamper for cover.

Continue along here until you turn right before a green kissing gate. Walk up two fields, then climb over a stile on the left and keep ahead again to a stile into the pretty churchyard, where daffodil and crocus nodding in the breeze, may welcome you to the church's oaken door.

Dedicated to St John the Evangelist, the building is light and airy, giving a feeling of peaceful spaciousness. Originally the church of the Ashton Hayes estate, it's now under the patronage of Keble College, Oxford.

As you walk down the nave look for the numbers on the pews, dating from a time when families rented their own seat. Notice too the misericord, an accommodating seat for the Vicar, allowing him either to lounge comfortably or prop himself upright.

The beautiful woodwork around the chancel was all carved locally, and each panel of the pulpit was worked by a different local craftsman. The round, wooden collection plate is also unique. Its twelve sections symbolise the twelve disciples, with one panel flawed to represent Judas.

Two Viennese crosses, carved into the surface of the altar table, were made by a well-loved parishioner blinded in battle — a poignant reminder of war's atrocity. And outside, the war memorial is another lasting tribute to those who died in the two World Wars.

As you leave the church notice the guild room — a hive of activity. The old school too across the road is another meeting place, and you may hear the playgroup as you pass the village institute. What struck me particularly about Ashton was the number of meeting places, all well used by the local community.

Turning right you soon reach the modern primary school.

The seat in the grounds is a 'Welcome Seat' where anyone may rest. Installed in 1983, the first to sit on it were the oldest past pupil and the youngest present pupil, together with the Mayor of Chester.

With its mellow walls and thatched roof, April Cottage is one of the oldest buildings in the village. Many years ago the lady who lived there had a counter inside the front door, behind which she sold sweets to the children from screw-topped jars. Oh, the delight and difficulty of spending that weekly sixpence!

After passing Village Farm, you may wish to wander down West End, which turns right opposite the *Golden Lion* — your journey's end.

Down here, Manor Farm stands opposite the parish room with its pointed door and windows. Before the church was built services were held here and it was called the mission room. At the end of this idyllic street an old cottage, with walls of wattle and daub, gives a final fillip to any walk around this pretty Cheshire village.

AROUND DELAMERE FOREST

Start: Tiger's Head (SJ 572 726)

Route: Tiger's Head - Town Farm - Flaxmere - The Carriers Inn at Hatchmere - Barnbridge Gates - Sandstone Trail to Eddisbury Lodge - Delamere Station - Harthill Bank - Norley Post Office

Distance: 8 miles

By Car: Take the A49 from Warrington. Turn right after crossing the River Weaver swing bridge. Turn left at the top of the hill, then right at Acton Bridge station. Immediately after passing Crowton Church turn left into Bent Lane, then right into Marsh Lane. Turn right again onto School Bank to reach the *Tiger's Head*, with its spacious carpark.

Tiger's Head
Tel: 01928 788309

Sited in Pytchley's Hollow, you will find a warm welcome at the *Tiger's Head* and nothing is too much trouble for the pleasant, efficient staff. Warmed by the comforting blaze of coal fires in Winter, the pub is open all day, every day, and food is served both at lunchtime and in the evening.

The half-timbered building, once a farmhouse, dates back to 1678 and the dutch barn next door has a preservation order on it. The farm eventually became a coaching inn and an overall-clad highwayman with thick grey hair is still reputed to haunt it. Nowadays, the *Tiger's Head* is a popular calling place for the local hunt, which gathers outside around the Australian oak, an uncommon evergreen shedding its leaves in June and July.

Traditional Real Ale from the Burtonwood Brewery is served, both mild and bitter, as well as a guest beer which changes regularly. Tea and coffee are also always available. Parties of ramblers and Treasure Hunts are welcome and a hot pot, or other food, can be laid on with prior notice. There's also a separate room for private functions.

The menu is extensive and so is the 'specials' board. All the dishes are home-made using fresh ingredients and local vegetables. Soup and a selection of sandwiches are readily available for anyone wanting a light snack and, on Sundays, a traditional Sunday lunch is served as well as a cold buffet.

For the energetic, there are pool and darts inside and a bowling green and children's playground outside. One local resident was disgusted with the youth of today though, when he erected the village stocks on the green opposite in May 1996 and penned the inscription ...

> *Donated as a deterrent to the young hooligans of the village who no longer have the discipline, respect or self respect expected of them by the community.*   *John S Astbury*

Hopefully, things have improved since then. Notice too the rusty, yellow Automobile Association sign on the bowls' pavilion, which states the mileage to London, Chester and Warrington from Norley and promotes Safety First.

Walk this way ...

Turn left out of the carpark and go down the snicket next to Rose Cottage. The path runs behind gardens until you turn left over a stile and cross a boggy area on planks. Then walk ahead, uphill, to a stile by a steel gate at the field's far end. Continue forward past the barns of Home Farm until you turn right, then left to a crossroads.

Home Farm is a good example of a Cheshire farmstead. The attractive, black-and-cream farmhouse, built in 1764, and the surrounding stable block, form a square around a cobbled courtyard — standard practice then to provide both shelter and safety for man and beast.

Walk ahead down Town Farm Lane, where there are other examples of Cheshire farms. You then pass behind Norley Hall and, when the road veers left, take the track to the right of *The Oranges*, then fork left straightaway.

Continue between hedge and sand quarry until you drop down to a tiny stream, which forms several pools along its course and is known locally as *The Fishponds*. Climb up the hillside ahead, negotiate the motorcross track and veer right to a stile in the fence before the entrance gate. From here, cross the field to a stile by a steel gate in the facing hedge and turn left down Beech Lane.

Turn left again onto Norley Road and, after passing Brownmoss Farm, turn right alongside farm buildings. Continue forward on a grassy track between fields, then walk down a snicket to a dirt road and carry on past Flaxmere to the picnic area, parking and toilets.

The reed beds at Reedsmere — a picture of peaceful tranquility.

The name, Delamere, means 'forest of meres' and on this walk it's easy to see how the area got its name. In the 13th century Flaxmere was a sheet of water, but it has slowly silted up until all that now remains is a sunken moss, an ideal breeding ground for dragonflies.

The *Carriers Inn*, overlooking Hatchmere's reed-fringed banks, may entice you inside before you continue beside the mere along Delamere Road (B5152). Where the water ends turn left along a path, which meanders through bracken and grassy clearings to the forest's edge. Cross one stream and turn left beside a second, following a boggy path to a wooden bridge, then climb uphill and turn right along a broad ride, its soft, springy surface strewn with pine needles.

Today, Delamere Forest covers 4,000 acres of Cheshire but, many centuries ago when the Ancient Britons camped here, it was three times as big, stretching from Nantwich to the River Mersey.

Turn right at a junction along another wide track, which leads to the edge of the forest and perhaps the sight of a sheep-strewn field. Do not turn left until you arrive at a stile (which you ignore) and turn back into the forest. Finally, keep ahead at a broad ride to reach the carpark and toilets at Barnsbridge Gates.

Many birds, including wren, nuthatch, jay and the tit family, are enticed into this landscaped gravel pit by food put out by the forest rangers.

Walk up the slope at the far end of the carpark and turn left along the Sandstone Trail. Keep ahead at the next fork, following the distinctive yellow markers which lead straight on both at the next crossroads and the following fork. As you cross the railway bridge it seems incongruous to hear the hoot of a diesel in this quiet spot.

Yet this is the busy Chester to Manchester line. Constructed in the 1870s, it was one of the few rail links built and owned by a committee — the Cheshire Lines. It was also the last line to be brought into British Rail in 1947 — six months after the rest owing to an oversight!

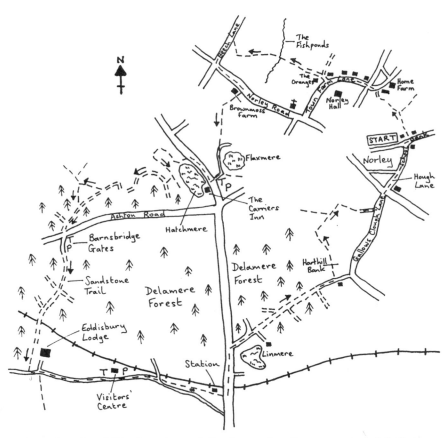

Keep ahead uphill, then bear right through a fence gap, and follow a stream, banked with bracken, until you turn left to the entrance of Eddisbury Lodge.

In the Middle Ages, Delamere was divided into the twin royal forests of Mara and Mondrem and became a popular hunting ground for the nobility. Eddisbury Lodge was well used by shooting parties at that time. Today it is noted for its Aberdeen Angus cattle.

The Sandstone Trail goes off to the right here as you keep ahead towards Linmere and Delamere Station.

Over to the right, Eddisbury Hill is the highest point of the area and has the remains of an ancient fortress on its summit.

The Forestry Commission took over the management of Delamere from the Crown in 1923 and you soon pass its largest nursery. Here, pine and spruce fir are started off, then grown on in plantations elsewhere in Britain, as the light, sandy soil of Delamere is not nutritious enough to sustain large trees.

The well stocked Visitors' Centre here is worth a visit. It's open every day from 10.30am until 4.30pm and has a welcoming, wood burning stove in Winter and picnic benches outside in Summer. Recently, its toilets have also won a Loo of the Year award!

Continue along the road to the railway bridge, then follow a dirt track parallel with the railway line. After passing cottages built for railmen you reach Delamere Station, where a café provides refreshments. Ascend the flight of steps ahead and turn left along the B5152.

Ignore the turn to Windyhowe Farm and take the next official right turn down a stony track, with Linmere gleaming far below. Keep straight on at a bend, walking round the barrier. Along here, pleasant clearings are dominated by the sturdy boles of massive beech trees, their shallow, tangled roots proving a menace to an unwary walker!

Keep ahead at a junction and stay on this wide, sandy track until you walk uphill and leave the forest on a bridleway. Where this veers right at New Pool Cottage turn left through a gate and walk down a grassy track, sheltered by Harthill Bank, where a hedgerow of ash, holly, hazel, dogwood, blackthorn and hawthorn has been newly planted.

Keep ahead at a stile by a stream, wending your way uphill on a tractor track which continues between hillocks. Then bear right along the facing hawthorn hedge, which eventually takes you onto a grassy track and into a small valley. Ascend out of this and turn right at the wood's far end, waymarked to Gallows Clough Lane. Continue beside a barbed-wire fence on a path composed of soft soil and leaf mould. Turn left along a rough road servicing houses, then left again along Gallows Clough Lane. Finally, keep ahead at the crossroads, down Hough Lane and School Bank, to return to the *Tiger's Head.*

AROUND KELSALL

Start: *The Boot Inn* in Boothsdale (SJ 531 672)

Route: Cat Lane - Castle Hill - King's Gate - Hanging Stone Hill - Stoney Lane - (Primrose Hill Wood) - Harrow Hill - Tirley Garth - Sandstone Trail - Willington Wood - Summer Trees Tea Room - Gooseberry Lane.

Distance: 8 miles (Short cut 6 miles)

By Car: Travelling east along the A54 from Chester, turn right at the traffic lights at the end of the Kelsall bypass. After passing the pub, *Th'ouse at Top*, turn sharp left uphill. Turn left again at a crossroads and look out for the *Boot Inn* sign on the left in 600 yards. The carpark is on the left at the top of this lane. The pub faces you, snugly hugging the hillside.

The Boot Inn
Tel: 01829 751375

The Boot Inn is situated in the Cheshire village of Willington, near Kelsall, close to the picturesque area known locally as *Little Switzerland*. This charming, long, low country inn was built as a dwelling house in 1815 and was subsequently bought by Samuel Prescott — a bag manufacturer from Liverpool. It was acquired by Greenall Whitley, the Warrington brewers, in 1913.

It is possible that *The Boot* originally got its name from the first four letters of Boothsdale. For many years, however, it was known as *The Cat*, perhaps after a local wag commented that a sign for the Red Lion, which a sign writer was painting in *The Boot*, looked 'more like a flaming cat'. Another story is that poachers on the nearby Willington

Hall estate were drinking in *The Boot* when lookouts warned that the gamekeeper was approaching. The gang hurriedly tossed their booty on the fire and, when questioned, swore it was the body of the inn's cat. The truth of these tales is uncertain but the lane which leads from *The Boot* is still called Cat Lane.

Joe Lloyd, thatcher, basketmaker and raconteur, became the landlord in 1931, and is still well remembered. Reluctant to mix ginger ale with whisky, prone to serving after hours and giving local girls wicker cradles as wedding presents, Joe, with Fluffy Nichols of Kelsall, featured in a local radio programme, which included numerous beeps to obscure the swear words! Long-standing regulars have other stories to tell!

An early attempt to promote tourism was made by Joe, who put up a sign for the Cyclists Touring Club (CTC) at the roadside, after which the inn became a popular rendezvous for teas, ale, and bed and breakfast. (The penny farthing made of pennies, on the wall today, provides a nostalgic reminder of this time.)

Over the succeeding years the one-room bar was extended by opening up the kitchen and then taking over the two adjacent cottages to create the very traditional country inn and restaurant which now serves a wide variety of home-cooked food, with mouthwatering 'specials' changed daily and a number of vegetarian dishes. There's also a selection of fine wines and guest ales from all over the country. *The Boot* is open for food every lunchtime and evening during the week and all day at weekends.

There is no music but you can be sure of a warm welcome and some lively conversation. Roast by open fires in Winter and, on long, sunny, summer days dine outside on the patio, then stroll across to see the rescued donkeys and pot-bellied pig in the adjacent field.

Walk this way ...

Leave the carpark with *The Boot* on your left, walking up the lane, which narrows to a footpath and shortly emerges into another lane. Turn left uphill between a field gate and hedge end, and westerly views soon open up to Tarvin and Chester.

You are now in Boothsdale, at the top of which is the site of Kelsborrow Castle, a Bronze Age fort, and 11 shallow steps, then 23 steeper ones, lead to a stile with a Sandstone Trail marker. Here, turn right along a barbed-wire fence to another stile by an iron gate.

 The Sandstone Trail is a long-distance footpath of 32 miles. It follows the central Cheshire ridge from Frodsham in the north to Grindley Brook, near Whitchurch, on the Shropshire border, and offers tremendous views across the Cheshire plain.

Glimpses of Kelsall can be seen before the next stile by a wooden gate, which takes you to a farm track bending right. Next, turn left over a stile before a metal bar gate, to reach an open grassy space by Lower Fold Cottage. Keep straight on from here to the road and a postbox. Turn right over the hill's brow, passing Delamere Farm, then the signpost for Primrose Hill Wood.

You are now standing at King's Gate, a reminder of the rigid forest boundaries when, from 1070 until the reign of Charles I, the Norman earls, then the Crown, ruled this forest, which once extended across much of Cheshire.

Turn left down a bridleway, with Primrose Hill Wood on your right, until you reach a signpost pointing back to King's Gate. Turn left here onto a wide path, with the forest boundary on your left. In 200 yards, at a Sandstone Trail sign, veer left onto the adjoining track, then fork left at another, similar post.

Primrose Hill Wood is a large, detached segment of Delamere Forest planted with a mixture of Scots and Corsican pine, with deciduous trees around its edge. Look out for grey squirrels, and birds such as willow warbler, chiff-chaff, tree-creeper and nuthatch.

At a junction and yet another post, this time with an orienteering mark, carry straight on over the hill's brow, then drop down to a corner stile. Keep ahead onto Primrose Hill, via a rough path bordered by Scots pine and scattered rocks, then climb over a double stile, noting the start of the Kelsall by-pass below. Walk alongside the babbling brook to a footbridge, then up steps to the carpark on Gresty's Waste. Take care as you cross the busy A54.

The twin buildings here are old toll houses. Also note the solid stone barn with ensuite pigsty (its thatch replaced by corrugated iron) and the outside feeding chute which kept fingers safe from hungry boars. There's also a mounting block for horse riders.

Go round the metal barred gate along a track to the signpost pointing right to a field stile.

From here you can detour left to find evidence of an ancient quarry, then use your imagination to decide which two rocks were the King's Chair and the one from which deer thieves were reputedly hanged — the origin of the name, Hanging Stone Hill.

Don't get too carried away before returning to the stile and following a wire fence to a new plantation — part of the Mersey Forest Project.

Part of the path along here follows the course of Watling Street, the Roman road joining Manchester (Mamucium) to Chester (Deva). Salt sent along here, from Northwich to the Chester garrison, was paid for in salarium (salt money) — the origin of our word, salary.

Enjoy the view over the forest while on this field path to Stoney Lane.

This junction must have been a crossroads way back in history. The hill with rocky outcrops behind the houses, is Eddisbury Hill, once an Iron Age fort and later (914AD) a Mercian fortress built by the Norse queen, Ethelfleda.

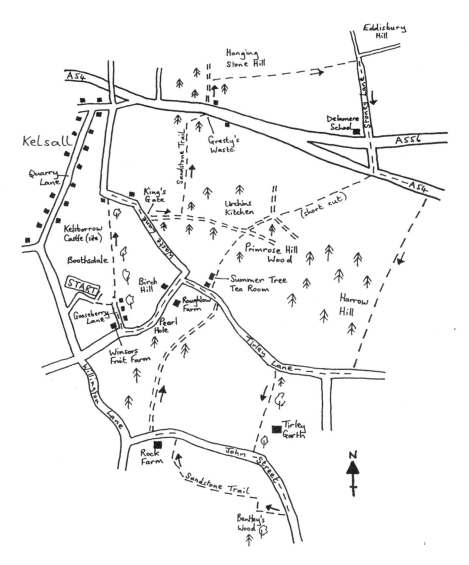

Turn right down Stoney Lane to reach the A556 at the village school.

An acre of land was given to Delamere by Queen Victoria for the erection of this school, which was built in the exact ecclesiastical centre of the parish and was opened as a national school in 1846. At a service to welcome home servicemen after the 2nd World War, the boys rang the bell so vigorously that the clapper flew off and has never been seen since. The bell now hangs inside the school as the belfry is unsafe.

Cross this busy road with care and keep ahead to the A54.

Short Cut ...

Cross the A54 to the field stile opposite, then walk diagonally across the field. If the path is not visible look up to the horizon and sight on the aerial tower until you see a track down to the forest edge. Climb over the stile here.

If you are curious about the Urchins Kitchen — a natural rocky cleft in the forest — turn sharp right from the stile along a rough track through the trees for about 150 yards. It's quite a surprise.

Back at the stile, walk uphill through Primrose Hill Wood, crossing a stone track and climbing to the forest boundary and another stile. Negotiate this and bear right to the hedge, turning up alongside it to a mini kissing gate.

Go through this and keep the hedge on your left. Climb over a stile and continue along a passage to the *Summer Tree Tea Room* (well worth a visit). Then continue to join the full walk at * as you turn right along Tirley Lane.

Full Walk ...

Turn left (east) along the main road. Walk on verges for 450 yards to a field stile on the right (not the stepped stile on the left). In the field follow the hedge on your left down into a dip and up to the forest boundary. This is Harrow Hill, and harrowing it is, a regular roller coaster, but just take it easy and enjoy the views, especially on the last part where, on a clear day, you can see beyond Northwich to Lostock Gralam and the chemical industry.

Turn right along Tirley Lane to the junction, then continue until you see a footpath on the left, to John Street. Turn down this, walking alongside Tirley Garth.

The beautiful grounds of this conference centre for the moral rearmament movement are sometimes open to the public.

Turn left along the lane until you turn right over a stile with a Sandstone Trail sign. Follow the footpath through Bentley's Wood, then enjoy the wide, open views all the way to Rock Farm. Turn left, then immediately right, still on the Sandstone Trail, and follow this sandy track until you turn left along Tirley Lane.

Both routes ...

Notice the house with a vertical sundial. Don't forget that it is unlikely to allow for British Summer Time and so may be an hour slow!

* Turn left at the junction with Waste Lane (a name associated with the local quarry) noting the weathered sign for Willington and Kelsall. Pass the 1894 mounting stone at Summer Bank Farm and notice the aerial navigation tower on Birch Hill. Round the bend the ground then falls steeply to Pearl Hole.

The spring and reservoir here are still connected to some of the older houses in Willington. The embankment is shored up with concrete cylinders, used as road blocks during the 2nd World War, then built up by German prisoners in 1944-46, who roughly inscribed the words DON'T LEAN OVER on the sloping section.

Lower down, where the lane turns sharp left at the sign for Winsors Fruit Farm, you turn right up Gooseberry Lane, gaining height and passing some elegant reconstructions, in particular Smithy Cottage.

Stonework from an old chapel was used for the garage but don't be fooled by the date, which is even earlier than the reign of William the Conqueror. It's 1901 upside down but is this also false?

Before long a signpost in the hedge points down the footpath back to *The Boot* and welcome refreshment.

Winsor's of Willington

This well-known local business is worth a visit for its soft fruits in season and its many varieties of home-grown apples, salads, vegetables, cut flowers, herbs and cottage garden perennials.

Willington *has a long tradition of fruit growing on its sheltered slopes. Rhubarb has always been particularly popular and look out for wild damsons in the hedgerows.*

AROUND LITTLE BUDWORTH

Start: Red Lion (SJ 598 653)

Route: Budworth Pool - Park Road - Coach Road - Little Budworth Common - Oulton Mill - Dogmore Lane - Oulton Lake - Little Budworth

Distance: 6.5 miles

By Car: Take the A54 from Chester towards Middlewich. Turn right onto the A49, then first left, and left again at the gates of Oulton Park. The *Red Lion* faces the church in Little Budworth village.

Red Lion

Tel: 01829 760275

The *Red Lion* is the most common pub name in England but there's nothing common about this hostelry, which has had a licence since 1797. This unspoilt village inn, with its blazing fire in Winter, makes everyone feel at home, although it is not particularly proud to have provided accommodation for the murderess, Ruth Ellis.

Food of excellent quality is served all day on Sunday and every other lunchtime and evening except Monday. The kitchen specialises in home-cooked dishes and uses seasonal, fresh vegetables at all times. The Sunday roast is a real treat and there's always a choice of vegetarian meals on the menu.

Robinson's traditional Real Ale is served and is renowned in the area for its excellent condition. A good selection of wine, including New World wine, is available by the glass or the bottle. Alcohol-free, low alcohol drinks and fresh coffee or tea are also on offer.

The pleasant bowling green, which overlooks the church, can be hired, either by groups or individuals. Walking parties can also be catered for. Please ring for details.

Walk this way ...

Turn right as you leave the pub car park, then go left down sloping Mill Lane to pass the end of Budworth Pool. Here, turn left over a waymarked stile and walk alongside the lake for a short way until you turn right over another stile. Cross two fields, then turn left down a sunken, green lane. A typical feature of the Cheshire countryside, this was the original drovers' road between Helsby and Oswestry.

At Park Road turn left, then right over a stile waymarked to Whitehall Lane. Yellow arrows point the way clearly as you cross the field to a stile to the left of a white house. Turn left to another stile, then cross the field diagonally, skirting the wood, to a gate in the farthest corner.

Turn right for a short way up a deep, sandy lane, lying snugly between hedge-topped banks, before turning left down a well-worn track. Where this forks keep left over a stream and walk uphill.

Watercress was once exported to London from here, ideal growing conditions being produced by the pure, clear water from Robin Hood's Well and the sandy bottom of the stream. The beds can still be seen, split into compartments to ease the work.

Wrought-iron gates and an avenue of limes lead off to White Hall, once the palatial home of the agent running the Oulton Park estate.

Turn right down the first path after White Hall, waymarked the Coach Road, and follow the wood's edge until you pass a pond and ascend to a converted farm. Then continue along the track to Beech Road and turn left to the Coach Road. Cross this and keep straight on.

The Coach Road was built in the 18th century as a long, straight drive up to the gates of Oulton Park, then a large country estate.

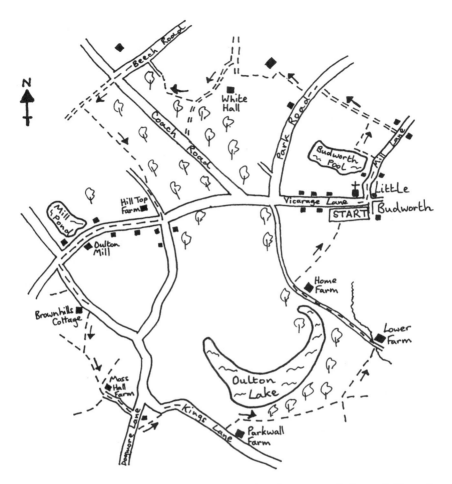

Keep on this track to the wood's end. Then turn left to follow its perimeter along a winding path until you eventually go over a stile on your right and continue in the same direction to Oulton Park School.

The sandy soil, in abundance in the large clearings of this lovely stretch of common land, has never been worth cultivating and the woodland, dominated by silver birch, has an almost ethereal quality.

Turn right along the road. The weather vane depicting fox with flaring brush stands out atop Hill Top Farm as you walk down to Oulton Mill and its attractive, reed-fringed mill pool.

Until gutted by fire this building had been converted from a flour mill into a thriving craft centre selling antiques and reproduction furniture. It is now a private residence and the mill pool, which once provided power for the wheel, remains a delightful feature.

Continue uphill, passing the Mill Pool Restaurant and a pleasant picnic spot, before turning left at the crossroads, towards Rushton. Immediately after passing Brownhills Cottage, attractively thatched and dating from 1675, turn right over a stile.

Cross the field diagonally and you will soon spot a stile in the facing hedge. Cross the following field diagonally too, to a stile in the hawthorn hedge. Again, walk diagonally up the next field to another stile, this time beside a steel gate, then follow the barbed-wire fence up to Moss Hall Farm. Keep ahead past farm buildings and down Moss Hall Lane, where a line of poplars act as a windbreak when a stiff breeze lashes across this predominantly agricultural area.

Notice the Victorian postbox as you reach Dogmore Lane and turn right, then left over a stile. Cross the two fields here to a corner stile onto Kings Lane, and turn right. After passing a wood turn left over a stile before Parkwall Farm. There's a good view of Oulton Lake and the motor racing circuit as you drop down to a crumbling wall.

Oulton Park is one of the premier venues for motor racing in England and has meetings on most weekends in Summer. The parkland boasts some of the finest lime trees in Cheshire, many over 200 years old, and larch, fir, beech and chestnut fringe the race-track.

Turn right beside the wall to the wood's end, negotiating six stiles, the last by a faded, white-painted gate, then follow the right-hand hedge to a stile and pretty stream. Turn left along the road, passing the Lower Farm of the Darley Hall estate and continuing alongside the stream, its banks awash with wood anemone and celandine.

Many footpaths radiate from the farms to the church tower as, in times past, the farmers used to pay their rent to the landowner there.

After passing Home Farm, its neat buildings grouped round a cobbled yard, turn right over a stile by an oak, its bole gnarled as an elephant's foot. Pass a telegraph pole before dropping down to another stile, then climb uphill to a facing stile between two gates.

Keep the hedge on your left as you continue over two more fields, then keep ahead down Booth Avenue to the main road (Vicarage Lane). Turn right here, passing the attractive Millennium Green and perhaps visiting the church on your way back to the *Red Lion*.

St Peter's Church

The oldest part is the tower. Thought to have been of secular origin, built as one of the beacons radiating out from Beeston Castle to warn of any imminent attack by Welsh raiders, this theory is supported by the unseemly behaviour of two hidden gargoyles!

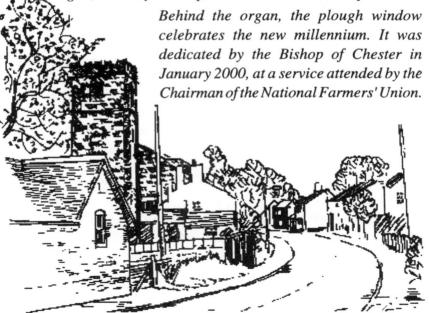

The light and spacious interior boasts the widest unsupported church roof in Cheshire. The acoustics are superb and the organ, made by Hill's, provides excellent accompaniment.

Behind the organ, the plough window celebrates the new millennium. It was dedicated by the Bishop of Chester in January 2000, at a service attended by the Chairman of the National Farmers' Union.

AROUND THE PECKFORTON HILLS

Start: Pheasant Inn (SJ 523 565)

Route: Haunted Bridge - Gospel Oak - Peckforton Hall - (Elephant and Castle) - Willis' Wood - Beeston Castle - Moathouse Farm - Outlanes Farm

Distance: 6.5 miles

By Car: Take the A41 from Chester. In Milton Green, turn left down Frog Lane. Drive straight through Tattenhall and follow signs to the *Candle Workshops* and Burwardsley. Turn left at the post office onto Higher Burwardsley Road. The *Pheasant Inn* faces you near the hilltop. Turn left to its carpark.

Pheasant Inn
Tel: 01829 770434

The *Pheasant Inn* is a 300-year-old sandstone and half-timbered building, nestling in the Peckforton Hills, with magnificent views over the Cheshire plain to Wales. Originally a farmhouse on the Carden Estate, the pub was first known as the *Carden Arms* and the restaurant at the back, which was the original farmhouse kitchen, still has its traditional cooking range. The charming lounge bar is bisected by the largest log fire in Cheshire and the conservatory and patio are a joy to use on summer days, when afternoon teas are served.

The inn has a well-earned reputation for mouth-watering food, with an original selection of delectable 'specials' always on offer. It also serves fine wines and a range of Real Ales from its well-stocked bar.

The Pheasant stands about half-way along the 32-mile Sandstone Trail, in some of Cheshire's most attractive countryside, and walkers are always welcome. En suite bed-and-breakfast accommodation is also available if you fancy staying overnight.

Walk this way ...

Turn right from *The Pheasant* and pass *Sunnyside* before turning right again, over a stile, and climbing steeply up through the wood. Negotiate a stile at the top, cross the field to another, then turn left along the lane. At Elephant's Track cottage turn left again to pass Hill Farm and walk under the Haunted Bridge.

The Haunted Bridge used to take carriages from Peckforton Castle to the gatehouse. According to local lore if you see a ghostly servant woman carrying her head under her arm you will be dead within the year. Cheerful thought!

Turn right over two stiles immediately after the bridge to see Peckforton village nestling below, with views over to the Pennine foothills on a clear day. Keep right along the sandstone wall for a short way before dropping down past two oak trees (one hollow), then walking beside a fence to a stile.

From here skirt to the right of a wood and overgrown quarry to the huge and gnarled Gospel Oak, beneath which John Wesley probably preached. Then drop down to the road through a pretty fir plantation.

Turn right along Stone House Lane, then immediately left at the crossroads down Peckforton Hall Lane, towards Bunbury. Pass Manor Farm and turn left just before Peckforton Hall, waymarked to Beeston and Bunbury.

Keep to the right of the fenced-in lime tree, then veer left before the Hall's entrance to walk alongside the fence, then a hawthorn hedge, where the full extent of the wooded Peckforton ridge is revealed. Keep along the farm track and enjoy a splendid view of the two castles, separated in age by several centuries.

Peckforton Castle is a superbly constructed sham. Modelled on a Norman castle, it was designed by Anthony Salvin and built in the 19th century. Locally-quarried sandstone was used throughout and it was to be the country seat of Lord Tollemarche.

Cross the tiny, meandering River Gowy and immediately turn left over a stile. Cross the field in the same direction as you've come. Negotiate the ditch at the far side, then veer slightly left across the next field, where a stile in the hedge leads onto the road.

Here you may wish to turn left for a short distance to see one of Cheshire's oddities in the garden of Laundry Cottage — a stone elephant and castle, originally built as a beehive.

Then turn back along the road until you see the lodge of Peckforton Castle on your left.

The room above the archway at the lodge used to house the local school. Opposite is an ancient oak, its trunk's girth measuring 21 feet.

Just before reaching the lodge climb over the stile in the hedge on your right, walking towards Beeston Moss and Bunbury. Cross the field diagonally, aiming for the left-hand edge of Willis' Wood until you spot the stile into it.

Follow the path through the wood, then pass the pond and keep ahead over the field to join the track to the right of the farm ahead. Cross this, go along a short track and turn left along the road. Pass an ancient cottage and Brook Farm, then follow the signs to Beeston Castle. Turn left at the junction, right at the cottage with the Victorian postbox and right again past a converted chapel.

Atop a high, craggy outcrop rising 300 feet from the plain below, Beeston Castle was built by Ranulf, Earl of Chester, in 1220, as a military stronghold to withstand the Welsh. Its turbulent history includes plenty of fierce fighting during the Civil War, when it was eventually captured by Roundhead troops.

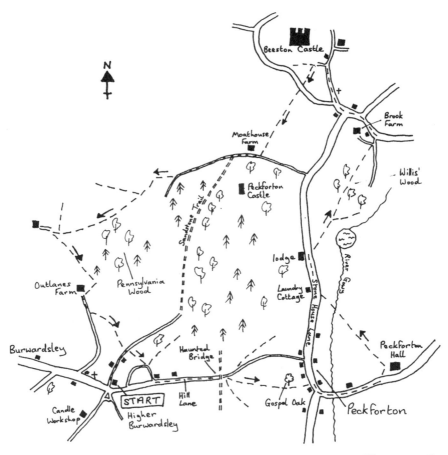

A steep climb from the outer walls takes you to a moat, still spanned by a drawbridge, and Richard II is reputed to have buried treasure worth almost £1m in the well — 370 feet deep. The view from the castle is stupendous, spanning eight counties on a clear day.

After visiting the castle turn right from the gatehouse, walking beside the castle wall to the public carpark and *Castle Snacks*. From here continue through a snicket, bear left at a fork and walk along the Sandstone Trail down through the wood. Cross the road and follow the path ahead (waymarked to Grindley Brook), over fields, a stream and another field. Then turn right onto a lane (waymarked to Bulkeley Hill) and you soon pass the attractive Moathouse Farm complex.

Keep ahead where the Sandstone Trail veers left into Peckforton Woods. (Daffodils line the lane in Spring and you pass pheasant rearing pens.) At the wood's end veer right diagonally across a field. Keep to the left of the telegraph pole at the far end, then walk beside the wood until you turn right along a path into it and cross a stream.

Cross a rubberised electric fence, then continue along the side of two fields, keeping the wood on your left. Turn right down through the wood, then left over two stiles separated by a stream. Keep ahead with the hedge on your left to a stile in the corner by the farm.

Bear left here to cross a ditch by a plank, then keep ahead over the facing field, making for two oak trees at the far end. Pass to the left of these, climb over a stile by a gate and drop down to cross another stream. Then walk alongside the wood and turn right over a stile. Leave this field by a corner stile, just past Outlanes Farm.

Turn left up the lane. At the end of the first field turn left over a stile — where the hedge angles left. Walk uphill, cutting off the corner, to climb over the stile at the top. Then turn right along the hedge to the lane, where you turn right again back to *The Pheasant*.

Pheasant Rearing

The *Pheasant Inn* is aptly named for each of the three large local estates rear birds in specially adapted pens. Waste Hill Farm, above Peckforton village, used to be called *The Pheasantry* when it was home to the Peckforton estate's gamekeeper.

Introduced to Britain by the Normans 900 years ago, the rearing of these unintelligent but attractive birds in this area now definitely takes precedence over forestry and the quarrying of local stone — once so prevalent here.

Shooting parties take place in the Autumn, when the cocks are shot and the hens kept for breeding. A popular custom is the day set aside as a shoot for the local farmers.

SOUTH CHESHIRE

Aston *Bhurtpore Inn*
One of the longest walks in the book, with plenty of interest along the
way — field footpaths, a canal, a pottery and an excellent village inn.

Hurleston Reservoir *The Barbridge Inn*
A waterways walk, with fields, lanes and a hostelry open all day.

Marbury cum Quoisley *The Swan*
A treasure of a village and a walk which
meanders around the meres and mounds of
the deep south's attractive countryside.

Mow Cop *The Ash*
This ramble has almost everything — industrial and spiritual history,
panoramic views, a canal, and the finest hall in England.

Wrenbury *Cotton Arms*
This walk was a real challenge to put together as, at the time of
writing, it involved using four *Pathfinder* maps. The Ordnance
Survey's new *Explorer* series may simplify this somewhat. The
route's worth following anyway, for it takes in Baddiley's tiny bethel
and the bascule bridges of the Macclesfield Canal.

A Place to Visit

Barn Books

Known as the *Bookshop in the Countryside*, fascinating titles fill three rooms of the barn at Pear Tree Farm to bursting point. This thriving business, in its idyllic situation, boasts one of the largest selections of books about Shropshire and Cheshire in the area, including both outdoor leisure and local history titles. There are also antiquarian and second-hand books, an interesting selection for children and volumes covering many other subjects — gardening, needlework, biography — you name it, they've probably got it.

Pear Tree Farm belonged to the Cholmondeley estate until 1913, when it was sold as a working farm, which it still is, with arable and wheat crops grown organically and a thriving dairy herd. The front of the farmhouse was rebuilt in 1830 and the back in 1894, when all the most up-to-date equipment for cheese-making was installed and the whey was even pumped under the yard to feed the pigs.

An ancient marker stone, complete with benchmark, goes deep into the ground, half-hidden in the grass at the front of the barn. In Summer, the greeny-white globes of huge angelica plants welcome you into the farmyard and cottage garden flowers spill over the cobbles with gay abandon.

Barn Books is open every Friday, Saturday and Sunday from 10am to 5.30pm, and on other days by appointment. (Tel: 01948 663742) Follow the directions for the start of the Wrenbury walk (page 100) and you will pass it on the left.

For any book lover a visit here is sure to be a total treat.

AROUND ASTON

Start: Bhurtpore Inn (SJ 609 471)

Route: Aston - Broomhall Green - Austin's Bridge - Shropshire Union Canal - Moss Hall Bridge - Hollin Green Lane - Hall 'o Coole - Hollin Lane - The Firs Pottery

Distance: 8.5 miles

By Car: Take the A530 south-west from Nantwich. After passing the village of Sound, turn right at a crossroads, signposted Aston. *The Bhurtpore Inn* is on the left in the village.

Bhurtpore Inn
Tel: 01270 780917

Once a part of the Combermere estate, the pub was originally known as the *Queen's Head*, then the *Red Lion*, until it became the *Bhurtpore Inn* in the wake of Lord Combermere's destruction of the great fort of Bhurtpore in India, early in 1826. Lord Combermere also celebrated his other great victory, at Salamanca in Spain, by naming a second local pub, close to the station, after it. Sadly, this has now closed.

In 1849 Joyce George, together with her immediate family, took over the running of the *Bhurtpore Inn* and Philip George, her grandson, bought the freehold in 1895 for around £850, when the Combermere estate was losing money. After renovation the inn was described in county records as the best run hostelry in the area.

In 1901, the *Bhurtpore* was bought by Woolf's Brewery of Crewe and eventually became a Tetley's pub. It was modernised again in the late 1980s but did not prosper and was then closed and boarded.

Late in 1991 Simon George (great, great, great grandson of Joyce) and his wife, Nicky, bought the pub free of tie for the first time in 90 years. Much work followed to refit the building and it reopened on 9th April 1992.

In the words of the landlord ...

"The emphasis of the 'new' *Bhurtpore Inn* is on traditional beers, fresh, home-cooked food and the welcoming atmosphere of a comfortable village local.

We offer an extensive choice of beers, with a constantly changing range of ten *Real Ales* from small, independent brewers. These all produce a plethora of innovative and traditional beers, often to tremendously high standards, but find outlets for their products extremely few and far between.

Most pubs, particularly in Cheshire, are tied to brewers or pub companies who dictate what will be sold. Even so-called 'Free' Houses are nearly always tied up, either through attractive loan agreements or discount deals. By retaining genuine freedom at the *Bhurtpore* we are able to sell only products that we feel are worthy of our stamp of approval.

We also stock many of Europe's finest beers, with five imported ones on draught and over 180 bottled beers, which include possibly the largest range of Belgian ales in Britain.

Pictures and artefacts which decorate the pub are also only used if there is some genuine relevance to the *Bhurtpore Inn*."

Bravo!

In recent years this dedication to quality has been rewarded by CAMRA who, in their *Out Inn Cheshire* guide to over 1000 pubs and bars in the county, awarded the *Bhurtpore* the title of *Best Pub in Cheshire*. It has also won the national *Beer Pub of the Year* award in Britain's best selling and independent *Good Pub Guide*.

Certainly this makes it a winner with those Cheshire bell ringers who consider themselves to be connoisseurs of *Real Ale*. The *Bhurtpore*'s Timmermans peach beer is also popular with the ladies, together with their real cider and perry.

Food is served every day, both at lunchtime and in the evening. An extensive 'specials' board has roast beef on offer every Sunday and there's a separate vegetarian menu. Finally, to further the Indian connection, the home-made curries and baltis are well worth sampling.

Walk this way ...

The area around Aston is still dominated by farming and Aston House Farm, opposite the inn, is one of the oldest farmhouses in the area.

From the *Bhurtpore*, cross the road to the opposite footpath and turn left. Just before a sharp left-hand bend turn right over a stile under an oak. Follow the fence on your right to a stile. Keep ahead, with the hedge on your right to the next stile, obscured in the field's far corner.

Continue in the same direction, crossing numerous stiles until you reach a green lane and then go through a white gate onto the A530. Cross over with care and turn left, to walk along this busy road, using the verge where possible. After crossing the River Weaver ignore a stile, then turn right along a lane towards Broomhall Green.

In late August a noisy mass of house martins were meeting on roofs and telegraph wires along here, perhaps planning their migration to Africa's warmer climes.

Turn left at a junction and, after passing Holly Bank, turn right down a track, walking under a high arch formed by firs to reach the Broomhall Riding School at Lynn Easton. From here, veer right at the first house to a stile and continue past the training area and the next field to another stile. Continue diagonally left down the next, long field to a stile in the ditch in the bottom corner. (There may be nettles!)

Keep straight on to the waymarker to the right of a forked, dead tree in the opposite hedge. From here you can see the next stile and waymark at the end of the facing hedge, where you climb over two stiles separated by a track.

Ahead is moated Mickley Hall and to your left the Trig point pillar.

However, your route is ahead at first, then right down to a South Cheshire Way sign in the field's far corner. Go over the stile beside the field gate here and bear left to the corner of a hedge. Then walk diagonally left down the field to a stile and gate in the far corner, and cross the next field alongside the left-hand hedge to a stile.

Now bear over to the right-hand fence and continue down it, passing a dried-up pond on your left. The waymarked stile out of this field is to the right of an oak. Next, keep along the right-hand hedge of the following short field to a stile hidden behind a blackthorn bush, covered with sloes in August. Finally, keep straight on to reach the Shropshire Union Canal at Austin's Bridge (No. 83).

Climb over a stile, cross the bridge, go through a white gate on the left, then walk under the bridge and along the towpath. You soon pass between the supports from an old railway track — a sheltered spot, home to a family of swans and a multitude of mallard ducks.

Continue along this delightful stretch of towpath, where wild flowers proliferate and redcurrants enhance the hedgerows. Beyond Moss Hall Bridge the first of Audlem's many locks can be seen, but you leave the canal here.

Walk up over the bridge, then negotiate a stile on the right. Walk towards the old brick building before dropping downhill (perhaps wading through wheat) parallel with the canal to a grey gate, a bridge over the River Weaver, then a stile. From here you can see the Moss Hall Aqueduct, which carries the canal over the river.

Climb up the field to a gate onto the dismantled railway line. Cross this and walk through the gate opposite. Keep ahead over this field, passing to the left of a clump of trees — once possibly a marlpit — to climb over a fence (a horse jump) in the corner of the hedge ahead with, thankfully, a yellow waymark.

Keep the fence on your right in the next field, negotiating two stiles at its end, then a copse of blackthorn and nettles, and another stile into the next field. Continue ahead alongside the neat, high hedge here to a stile in it, followed by a bridge and a stile into the facing field.

Veer diagonally left across this field (passing an oak on your right) and look for a stile in the electric fence at the start of a line of oaks. Walk in the same direction to a stile in the top hedge (behind a yellow tube round an electric wire, and well before houses on the right).

Cross the quiet lane and negotiate the rusty gate ahead, which might be open. Walk up this huge field, along the hedge at first, then veering right to make for a kink in the facing hedge. Walk down this to stiles and a bridge over the deep ditch.

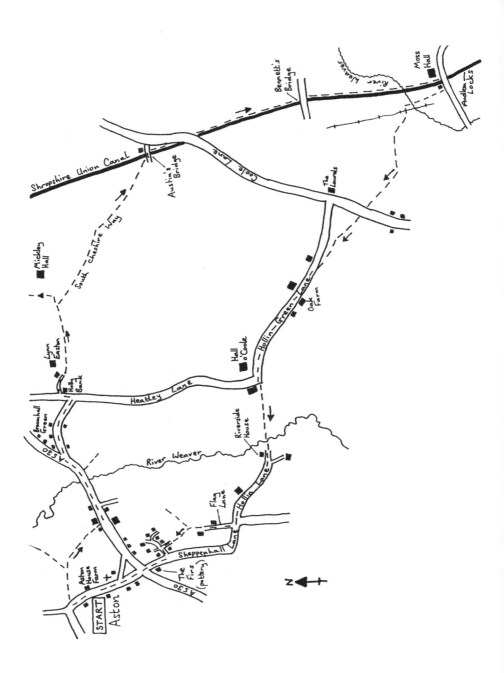

Shropshire Union Canal

Bennett's Bridge

Moss Hall

River Weaver

Audlem Locks

Coole Lane

Austin's Bridge

South Cheshire Way

The Laurels

Mickley Hall

Hellin-Green Lane

Oak Farm

Lynn Eaton

Hall o'Coole

Holly Bank

Heatley Lane

Broomhall Green

A530

Riverside House

River Weaver

Flag Lane

Hellin Lane

Sheppenhall Lane

Aston House Farm

The Firs (pottery)

A530

START
Aston

N

In the next field walk diagonally right to a stile in the hedge, on the far side of a house. Turn left along Hollin Green Lane, passing Hollin Green Farm and Oak Farm. At a sharp, right-hand bend enjoy the view of moated Hall o' Coole before walking straight on into the stableyard of Hall o' Coole Grange, a high Dutch barn conversion, where a warning sign cautions, 'This house is guarded by shotgun three nights a week. You guess which three!' Yappy terriers may snap at your heels as you hurry to put two stiles between you and them.

Follow the left-hand hedge to another waymarked stile in a barbed wire fence, then continue to an iron gate in the hedge corner. From here bear slightly right to cross a footbridge, then walk up to a broken iron gate which leads onto a lane at Riverside House.

Keep ahead to pass Hollin Lane Farm, then turn right at the junction down Sheppenhall Lane and immediately right again down a track (Flag Lane). After passing a cottage on the right and going through a gate, turn right over a stile. From here, stay in the same direction beside the fence, then past a long shed. **Don't** go over to a stile on your right, instead cross a plank bridge on your left and veer left to a stile hidden under an oak and holly.

Walk straight across the field ahead, keeping to the left of a house's large conservatory, where a wooden kissing gate stands between hawthorn and sycamore. Continue ahead along the road, then turn left down Sheppenhall Grove and right along Sheppenhall Lane again, to *The Firs* — a pottery.

*If open, **The Firs** has a selection of both functional and decorative pots for sale at prices to suit all pockets. Their stock ranges from salt pigs and puzzle spheres, to casseroles, clocks and coffee pots. Workshops are also held each week for both adults and children. (Tel: 01270 780345)*

Cross the A530 and continue back into Aston village.

AROUND HURLESTON RESERVOIR

Start: The Barbridge (SJ 615 566)

Route: Bremilow's Bridge - Trig Point - Cherry Orchard - Vicker's Bridge - Hurleston Reservoir - Fields Farm - Bullsgreen Farm - Mill Pool Lane

Distance: 5.5 miles

By Car: Take the A51 north-west from Nantwich towards Tarporley. Turn right after passing Hurleston Reservoir, then immediately left to park either in the pub carpark or on waste ground further down the road.

The Barbridge Inn
Tel: 01270 528443

Originally called the *Kings' Arms*, at one time *The Barbridge* was an old coaching inn on the main route from London to Chester. The dilapidated building opposite, once a fine stable block, has recently been demolished to make way for new housing.

In earlier times the Shropshire Union Canal, which runs right past the door, was a-bustle with the transport of coal and clay, linking North Wales with the Midlands and Manchester. Today it is almost as busy with pleasure boats.

The inn was refurbished and extended in 1987 and 1998 but still has its original cellar. At one time the different areas in the pub were known as locks; the top lock was the restaurant and the two bars were the middle lock and bottom lock. These names have now lapsed but the walls are still covered with a fascinating collection of maps, paintings and photographs linked to the canal. Aga stoves, and black-leaded cast iron ranges complete with bread ovens, also feature.

From the small, sunny conservatory parents can keep an eye on their offspring outside, where the play area's sturdy equipment provides for action and adventure. There's also a special children's menu.

The outside barbecue is popular in Summer, whenever, if ever, the sun shines! On hot, sunny days food is served outside, where many tables border the canal banks, and up a short flight of steps inside, the attractive, non-smoking restaurant also overlooks the waterway.

All the food is fresh and home-baked. There are many vegetarian dishes on the rotating menu and the vegetables are fresh, in season and steamed. The extensive 'specials' board has everything from farmhouse favourites to oriental dishes, and there are pensioners' 'specials' and suggestions for those with lighter appetites. The selection of delicious puddings may also include such mouth-watering delights as waffles with honey and ice cream, or chocolate torte with raspberry coulis and cream.

Five cask ales are on offer and guest beers which Real Ale buffs come from far afield to sample. However, there's no mild nowadays or North Pole lager! (Don't be fooled by this, it was only ice and water.) The high quality wine portfolio includes champagne, and you can buy by the glass or the bottle.

The fact that *The Barbridge* is open all day, every day, for food and drink is a major bonus. Parties are asked to ring prior to arrival and walkers can park in either of the carparks.

Walk this way ...

Walk back past the pub and turn left over Bremilow's Bridge, enjoying the sight of brightly painted barges lining the canal banks. Continue down the country lane, crossing the stream and passing Stoke Hall before turning right down the side of a field just before the drive to Stoke Hall Farm.

Keep ahead across the field, exit through gates, then walk between a barn and pond. After passing the slurry store, bear right in the field ahead to stiles into the next one. Cross this diagonally left, making for an oak, under which there's a plank bridge. Next, go through a small gate and veer right to two stiles and further planks.

Turn left up the hedge of the next field to a stile, then go ahead again up the following field, turning right at its end. (To see the trig point, its bench mark of S2728 denoting the highest point of this flattish area, negotiate a stile on your left. The newly-planted area here includes rambler rose, oak and rowan.) Retrace your steps, walk down the side of the field and cross the concrete lane to Gates Farm.

Keep ahead down the side of the next field to stiles, separated by planks over another ditch. Then bear right over the stile in the hedge and turn left, perhaps between a hawthorn hedge and sweetcorn — a long, sheltered stroll which eventually takes you round an ash-fringed pond to a stile in the facing hedge.

Bear diagonally right in the next field, to a stile by a steel gate, then turn left down a wide, stony track to a stile and gateway onto the lane to Cherry Orchard Farm. Cross this, keep ahead through a little gate by a cattle grid, then down the gravel drive of a pretty cottage and over the lawn to a stile behind a hole cut in the leylandii hedge.

This is a delightful cottage, its mellow brick walls lying low and snug in the pretty garden, where sleek-catkinned pussy willow spread wide their tortuous branches near the cherry orchard.

Keep ahead through the nettle patch to a stile. Rights-of-way run all round the sides of the next field except the side you want! To avoid walking in an unnecessary V, you may possibly be allowed to cheat and turn right alongside the hedge, passing in front of the three-storey Victorian farmhouse.

Turn right over a stile here and walk behind buildings to another stile by a gate-gap. Continue in the same direction down to a stile by a

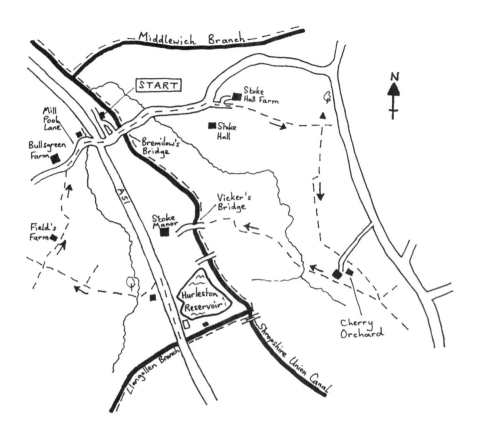

bridge. Cross this, then bear right, parallel with the meandering stream, until you see a stile in the facing fence — to the left of a thick hedgerow. Cross a second stile here into the next field.

Continue, with the hedge on your right, until you pass through a muddy gap (with hidden stile) into the next field. Keep along the hedge again until you go over a stile in it by an iron gate and walk beside a fence on your left. Turn left at its end and walk up the next field all the way to a stile onto the canal towpath at Vicker's Bridge.

The massive bulk of Stoke Manor is visible behind its transparent screen of trees, its huge chimneys looming above the foliage.

Walk along past Hurleston Reservoir, well hidden atop grassy banks.

Many birds take refuge on this large reservoir, especially during a hard Winter when it is the only unfrozen water for miles around. It's home to over fifty coots, as well as great-crested grebe and tufted duck, while Canada geese over-winter here and golden eye have also been spotted.

Look out for coots with their comical legs!

A welcome seat under a sturdy signpost pointing to Birmingham and Chester may allow you to bask in the warm afternoon sun before turning right over Bridge 97. Then continue along the Llangollen branch of the Shropshire Union Canal.

Planks are stored at many of the bridges, including this one, in case of a breach in the canal's banks or bottom. And from here you walk alongside an interesting series of four locks, separated by basins which allow drainage and repair work to take place in the winter months. There's also a lock-keeper's cottage and a hut opposite, where a keeper can rest and shelter. Notice too the overflow from the reservoir and the view of it from above the cottage.

At Bridge 1 walk under both new and old bridges before turning left up steps. At the top, turn left again and walk along the busy A51. After passing a lay-by, then byres and tyres, turn left down a short track which doubles back. Negotiate a stile and turn right, passing through two gates, then walking down a cart-track which veers right over a stream, then rises and continues through another gate.

As the track peters out continue along the hedge, then through the left-hand gate into the next field. Keep ahead again until, at the facing hedge, you need to negotiate your way over the water trough.

Walk ahead across the next field until you spy a rusty gate in the right-hand hedge — to the left of an oak. Walk across and exit through this, then continue over the field ahead, keeping to the right of Field's Farm —attractively restored from a ramshackle ruin.

Pass through the gateway into the next field, then veer left along a grassy track. Stay on this all the way to Bullsgreen Farm, where a stile and a very mucky area leads to Mill Pool Lane. Turn right along this, crossing a pretty, fast-flowing stream on the way to the A51.

Cross this busy road with care and continue up another section of Mill Pool Lane. A final left turn, down Old Chester Road at the tiny, modern Methodist chapel, takes you back to *The Barbridge* and journey's end.

AROUND MARBURY CUM QUOISLEY

Start: The Swan (SJ 562 458)

Route: Marbury - Big Mere - Wicksted Hall - Quoisley - Shropshire Union Canal - Little Mere

Distance: 5 miles

By Car: Marbury is three miles north of Whitchurch and the winding country lane leading to it is signposted off the A49. Park at *The Swan*, or nearby where the road widens.

The Swan

Tel: 01948 663715

Fronting this picturesque pub is a typically English village green where, on a hot summer's day, welcome shade spreads out from a massive oak. Planted in 1814 to commemorate Wellington's victory over Napoleon at Orthes, its trunk is denuded of bark on one side where it was struck by lightning. A mistle thrush finds it safe enough to live in though and makes frequent sorties to the orange-berried pyracantha on the pub's front wall.

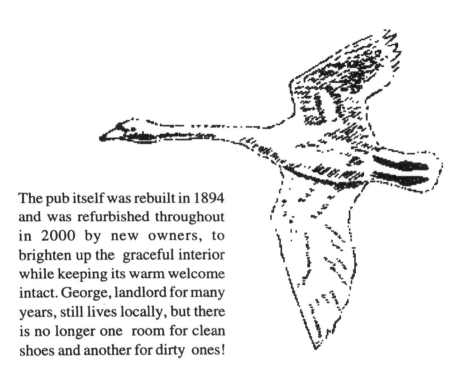

The pub itself was rebuilt in 1894 and was refurbished throughout in 2000 by new owners, to brighten up the graceful interior while keeping its warm welcome intact. George, landlord for many years, still lives locally, but there is no longer one room for clean shoes and another for dirty ones!

Walkers are welcome everywhere, but please ask first before using the carpark before walking. There's always someone around.

The Swan has an excellent reputation for good food, with folk travelling from as far away as St Helens and Wirral to sample the ample fare. The pub is not open on Monday lunchtime but on every other day is well worth a visit, with food served from noon until 2pm and in the evenings.

All the food is freshly cooked and the menu caters for vegetarians. The fish dishes, and sauces served with chicken, are changed regularly on the varied lunchtime menu, and the evening menu alters weekly. There's also a selection of mouth-watering sweets — all home-made. The dining room is non-smoking, children are always welcome — if well behaved! — and outside, there's a pretty patio and garden.

There's *Real Ale* from Tetley and Bass, together with a guest beer. *Weetwood*, from Willington near Kelsall, is popular.

Walk this way ...

Leave the pub carpark and turn right up the village street.

This area used to be called Grosvenor Square — a somewhat pretentious name perhaps for a village centre! The white barnlike building on your right used to be the stables for the local estate, with one end occupied by the stableman.

The cottages opposite were the homes of estate workers and the front walls still retain their original wattle and daub. One of them was the village shop for a while and a huge barrel stood by the door. Before the 2nd World War, the cottagers used to take in Liverpool children for a week's holiday each year.

Turn left to visit the church.

St Michael's Church*, built of red sandstone in perpendicular style, tops a knoll above the village. Its lychgate, erected to honour those who fought in the 1st World War, bears the poignant words:*

> *Ye who live on, mid English pastures green,*
> *Remember us, and think what might have been.*

Gaze up at the church's ornate battlements and pinnacles, and notice the gargoyles on the tower — smiling twins, mischievous monkeys and funny faces jokingly carved by medieval masons.

The church at Mellor boasts the oldest pulpit in Cheshire but the one here is runner-up. Dating from the 15th century its octagonal shape is deceptively simple. Another ancient relic is a wooden bier. Made by Robert Green of nearby Norbury in 1918, it is still used occasionally.

Leave the churchyard by the gate behind an ancient, chained but lifeless yew. Legend says that when it falls so will the church. Hopefully this won't happen, although subsidence is a problem.

Keep the hedge on your left as you drop down the field to the stile at the bottom, then turn right along the road towards Whitchurch.

This road used to be called Threadneedle Street and the second cottage has a window high up in its side wall. A tailor had it inserted to give him extra light as he sat cross-legged at his sewing. He also owned the first sewing machine in the district. This cottage also acted as the village store and post office at one time, when the postmistress used to get paid £6 a year! And in 1914, the village's first telephone was installed here.

Turn right through a small gate and drop down towards Big Mere, where you turn left over a stile.

On your left, a venerable oak has a trunk hollow enough for ten children to fit inside. On your right, the placid surface of the mere's clear water is ruffled by swans as they sail majestically along, but the peaceful scene is shattered dramatically by the loudly honking Canada geese. A pair of great crested grebe also nest here, together with ruddy duck and many other waterfowl.

You have a good view of Marbury Hall before passing through a gate and along a bridleway, which may be muddy and leads to a further gate. Then continue beside the wood, with its tangled mass of undergrowth, to a stile.

Bear slightly right, walking up a slight indentation to a stile beside a gate, then keep slightly left as you cross the following, huge field, to reach another stile by a small gate. Keep to the right of trees as you ascend another massive field, then veer right to a stile, which separates a hedge and fence.

Climb over this and turn left along the hedge to Wicksted Hall — now a Salvation Army Eventide Home. There's no need to go over the stile onto the road here. Instead, walk along the hedge to the next stile.

This is the highest point of the walk and the extensive views stretch over the hummocky, sheep-strewn fields of this fertile, farming area, to the meres at Quoiseley and the steeply rising hills beyond.

Walk down the field, parallel to the hedge on your left — the road a field away. Pass through a large gap in a facing hedge, then keep in the same direction over the next field, to a stile in the far corner in front of Deemster House.

Turn left to Wirswall Road which, like so many lanes in this area, gently winds through the countryside. Turn right along it for a short way before going left at an almost hidden signpost, which points you through a small spinney of hawthorn and rose.

The hedgerows around here are a diverse mixture of hawthorn, hazel, holly, hornbeam, blackthorn and sycamore, often interwoven by sweetly scented honeysuckle, and the grassy verges are awash with wildflowers such as foxglove, yarrow and knapweed.

Emerging from the spinney at a stile, follow the fence on your left for a very short way before crossing the field diagonally, climbing up to the far right. On the way pass two trees and a lone oak, then make for a pylon on the hilltop. Behind this a stile takes you down onto Wirswall Road again.

Go ahead down the lane, passing a huge ash and the track to Mere Farm on the way to Quoisley Hall, its ancient barn still topped by picturesque black-and-white eaves. Then, after rounding a corner, turn left over a stile.

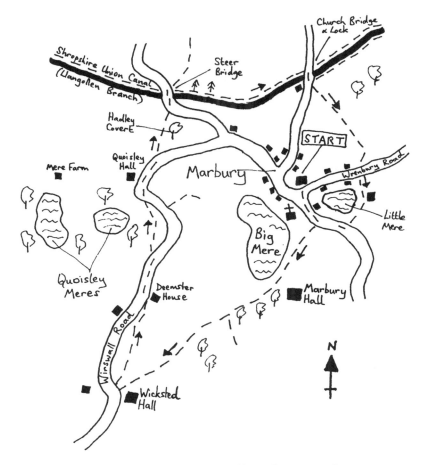

Make for the left-hand end of Hadley Covert, where you cross another stile and walk along the side of a wood, in May thickly carpeted with bluebells. Leave this by a further stile and walk straight over a field, passing a telegraph pole on your right. A stile then takes you onto a country lane and you turn left to Steer Bridge.

This is the Llangollen branch of the Shropshire Union Canal and, in the heyday of canal traffic, there was a busy wharf here, dealing with goods for the surrounding area. Animal feed and seeds were brought in and local farmers sent their Cheshire cheese to market by canal, as the water cooled the cheese.

Turn left off the bridge, then left again onto the towpath in the direction of Marbury. Along here grey squirrels may be cavorting in a coppice of larch or in the grotesquely-shaped, ivy-shrouded trees on the opposite bank. Leave the canal at Church Bridge and Lock, turning right up School Lane and immediately left over a stile.

Cross the field to a stile between gates, then follow a line of trees — the only remains of a hedge — up across the next field and continue to a stile in the facing hedge. In the following field bear right to the hedge and keep alongside it to a corner stile. Keep the hedge on your left in the final field, to reach Wrenbury Road. (If you need to take a short cut from here turn right back to the village.)

In Marbury, Wrenbury Road was once called Bulgaria Street — a fanciful name if ever there was one! Here lived a wheelwright who was also a keen, local bellringer — for the church has six bells, five of them cast by Rudhall of Gloucester in the 18th century.

Off Wrenbury Road, a little lane once led to a communal bakery and the modern house built on the spot is named The Old Bakehouse. Nearby, is Smithy Cottage, although the smithy itself was actually on the opposite side of the road, and when the post was only delivered from Whitchurch once a week letters were put in its window for villagers to collect.

To complete the full walk ... cross the road and go through the steel kissing gate opposite. Then keep ahead close to the hedge, passing through another kissing gate to reach the farm.

At one time this farm used to supply milk for the village. Responsible schoolchildren collected the milk in cans after school, the ha'penny per journey supplementing their meagre pocket money.

As you continue along the farm track you get pleasant glimpses of Little Mere through the trees, where a pair of swans may still nest and, as soon as the cygnets are old enough, shepherd them across the road to Big Mere. At the road, turn right back to *The Swan*.

Marbury cum Quoisley

This pretty village, its cumbersome title distinguishing it from the Marbury near Northwich, has stood amid the bumps and basins of southern Cheshire since Anglo-Saxon times. It's curious how the retreating Ice Age left behind this knobbly, sandstone area, the dips filled in by reed-fringed meres. Marbury is also the meeting place of several narrow lanes, which gently meander around the contours .

At one time Wakes used to take place on the village green during October, with dancing bears, barrel organs and coconut shies. Today, Merry Days in May have taken their place, with dancing and dog shows, raft races and motor launch trips on Big Mere, crafts in the village hall and a flower festival in church.

The villagers can also be justifiably proud of their many wins in the annual 'Best Kept Village' competition, as the wall of the white barn by The Swan testifies.

Part of this walk follows the **South Cheshire Way** which stretches from Mow Cop to Grindley Brook. This easy, lowland route is mainly rural and passes through many attractive villages. It links the southern end of the *Mow Cop Trail* to the southern end of the *Sandstone Trail*.

AROUND MOW COP

Start: The Ash (SJ 857 569)

Route: Chapel Bank - High Street - Mow Cop - Old Man of Mow
- Hanging Wood - Ackers Crossing - Macclesfield Canal
- (Little Moreton Hall) - The Hollow - Rockside

Distance: 5 miles, or 7 with the detour to Little Moreton Hall

By Car: Take the A34 south from Congleton. Turn left in Scholar
Green and, at first, follow the signs for Mow Cop, then
keep right up Birch Tree Lane to Mount Pleasant. Stay on
this road, climbing up Chapel Street until you reach *The
Ash*'s carpark on the right.

The Ash

Tel: 01782 513167

The Ash features in the *Le Routier* guide, has
magnificent views and is aptly named, its ash tree
lightly shading the carpark. A football field and play area slopes away
and, behind the pub, supposedly the oldest building in Mow Cop has
been converted into the footballers' changing rooms. That the pub
was extended into the adjoining cottage at some time in the past, is
evident both from the outside and the load-bearing beam inside.

What first attracted our family to *The Ash* was its superb Sunday
carvery, on offer from noon until 6pm — a godsend for walkers who
get up late! (This inn may just be in Staffordshire, but then boundaries
are often moved for one reason or another!)

The pub serves no food on Mondays in Winter, but on other weekdays
there is an *à la carte* menu and a 'specials' board, from which meals
can be ordered from noon to 2.30pm and 7 to 9pm. The food is home-

made, steak-and-ale pie and home-made soup being particularly popular, and the dining room has a 'no smoking' area. *The Ash* also has two traditional hand-pulled bitters and one guest beer always on tap.

About Mow Cop ...

Its unusual name comes from the Welsh or Celtic, *Moel*, and the Anglo Saxon *Cop*, meaning cap, and this prominent hilltop, which rises to a height of 1,100 feet, has been a focus of both spiritual and secular significance for about 1,000 years. Both the 'castle folly' and the nearby *Old Man of Mow* rock feature were given to the National Trust in 1926 by Mr Joseph Lovatt.

Mow Cop is at the southern end of a gritstone escarpment which starts at Congleton Edge and rises to 170 feet above sea level. The county boundary of Cheshire and Staffordshire also lies along the top road, which affords spectacular views.

The View and Landmarks

North:	Macclesfield Forest and Alderley Edge
North West:	Giant telescope at Jodrell Bank
West:	Beeston Castle and Welsh hills
South West:	Shropshire hills
South:	Industrial potteries
East:	Biddulph Moor and Peak District beyond

Walk this way ...

Cross the road outside *The Ash* and ascend the steep footpath opposite, to Chapel Bank.

To the right stands the old Wesleyan chapel. Built in 1852, it is now a local history museum, open every afternoon except Monday and Tuesday from May to September. There is a small admission charge.

Turn left along Chapel Bank and continue along High Street to the village shop and post office.

To the left stands the Primitive Methodist chapel — a huge barn of a place and very visible from the valley below.

In the wall below the shop is Parson's Well — one of several natural springs bubbling up from the earth on Mow Cop, which once provided the only water supply. They were covered and enclosed almost in cupboards to keep the water clean and this one, which dates from 1857, is carved with a Celtic cross and the inscription, 'Keep Thyself Pure'. There were also communal bread ovens nearby, where people baked on a rota system.

Stay on the High Street to the Mow Cop carpark on the right.

Primitive Methodism originated on Mow Cop one Sunday in May 1807, when several thousand people, organised by William Clowes and Hugh Bourne, a carpenter, gathered here. Nicknamed 'ranters', they wanted a simpler form of worship and this meeting proved to be the turning point, after which they were expelled from the more orthodox Wesleyan Methodism. Five years later their first chapel was built nearby, in Tunstall.

To commemorate the occasion a simple stone was unveiled on the slopes of Mow Cop by the President of the Methodist Conference in 1948. It can be seen in the Mow Cop carpark, inscribed with a hymn that is sung at the annual meeting still held here each year:

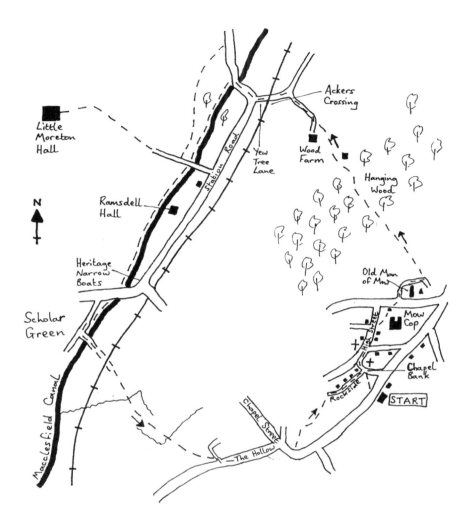

'Sing glory hallelujah the Lord is with us still,
The little clouds increasing that arose on Mow (Cop) Hill.'

From the Mow Cop carpark follow the sign pointing to the *Gritstone Trail* and Rushton Spencer, up a rough path. Then bear left at a fork in front of the 'castle folly'.

The 'Castle Folly' *was built in 1754 by local stonemasons, John and Ralph Harding, for Randall Wilbraham of Rode Hall. The ruined* *section of wall was a false feature, adding to the building's dramatic effect when seen on the skyline from the hall, three miles to the west.*

The tower originally had two floors and was used as a summer house and the roof was built as an inverted cone which could be used as a beacon. One may have been lit as part of the ancient tradition of celebrating Lammastide (1st August), which later led to the celebration of the Mow Wake, an event which continued into the 19th century.

Turn left along a track in front of a house, then right at the road and immediately left to the *Old Man of Mow*. Drop down the track before the bungalow here, then turn right along a tiny path between heather, willow herb and bramble, which leads to the base of the *Old Man* — the trig point standing guard high above.

The Old Man of Mow, approached from this angle, and with a little imagination, does indeed seem to have the profile of a face. This 70-foot high chimney is a natural rock formation left standing as a monument by the quarrymen of the 17th century. Local historians also believe this area was the site of a cairn and ancient burial chamber similar to the one at the Bridestones, south of Bosley Cloud.

Continue along this path, then turn right along the main track, enjoying stupendous views over to Jodrell Bank and the radio masts on Croker Hill.

After passing a house, turn left down a tiny, overgrown path to a stile. Then continue down the side of two fields, with views over to Shutlingsloe's prominent peak, and the nearer wooded slopes, and bare, rounded crown of Bosley Cloud resembling a balding man.

Climb over the stile into Hanging Wood and follow a well-marked, rocky path, which can also be muddy, down between bracken, bramble and bilberry, then beneath a darkly forbidding arch of holly. At the path's end look out for a stile on your left into a field.

Continue downhill on the high ground to the left of gullies. After passing an oak look for a marker post on the right, then continue between clumps of gorse to a rough fence followed by a holly hedge. At the end of this continue downhill on flattened grass between rising ground, passing under power lines and to the right of sycamores, to reach a small gate in a fence.

Continue on a downhill path, turn left along a track, right at a junction and left at a country lane, which takes you down to Ackers Crossing. Cross this main railway line with great care. It has very fast trains; look both ways and don't linger.

Walk down Yew Tree Lane with semi-bungalows on your right, then a right turn at a road junction takes you to bridge number 85 on the Macclesfield Canal. Cross this, descend steep steps on the right and turn right under it. Continue along the towpath to bridge 86.

From here you should be able to climb over a stile on the right, in order to follow the track, then negotiate several stiles and gates, to reach Little Moreton Hall. The distance is one mile. Retrace your steps after your visit.

Little Moreton Hall is well worth the detour. Dating from the 15th century, it's possibly the best example of a half-timbered, moated manor house in England. Guided tours take place on most afternoons between March and November and refreshments are served in the tea shop. (Tel: 01260 272018)

Continuing along the towpath, you soon pass Ramsdell Hall, then look out for an old stone milepost, showing Marple 25 and Hall Green 4. After passing the marina of Heritage Narrow Boats and sandstone bridge 87, the canal narrows briefly and there's a cottage — once the *Bird in Hand* pub.

Leave the canal on the outskirts of Scholar Green, through a gap in the hawthorn hedge just before bridge 89. Walk up the road here and turn left over the bridge. Continue ahead under the railway, negotiating unusual iron stiles.

Keep ahead again over a field to a stile at the start of a woodland path. Along here, the stream ripples far below and a stile into a field on the left may enable you to walk parallel to the very muddy path in wet weather. At the wood's far end, exit over a stile and continue forward across the field, with an excellent view of Mow Cop, the village clustered around the 'castle' like chicks round a mother hen. The huge, Primitive Methodist Church is also very visible on the hillside.

Part-way across the field bear left up the slope to a bridge high above a stream, which trickles down to join the one in the valley bottom. Keep in the same direction diagonally across the next, large field, on rising ground all the way to a stile in the far corner, then turn left up the road known as *The Hollow*.

Just before *High View* turn right up a footpath, which rises to a road. From here, bear right and immediately left, over a stile and along a narrow path. It doesn't matter whether you veer right or left along it as both paths end up at a blue gate, to the left of and above the outcrop. (Turning left may provide the easier option as the tiny path winds uphill to cross a tumbledown wall and fence, then continues, ever upwards, with far-reaching views.)

Pass the blue gate then, at a standing stone and path junction, turn left. At a house turn right and keep ahead (not left) at the wall's end, to walk along a rocky ridge with more stunning views. Continue behind a bungalow and up a stony track, then on along tarmaced Rockside. At Chapel Bank, turn right, then immediately right again (before the chapel) and retrace your footsteps down the steep path to *The Ash*.

The *Mow Cop Trail* stretches for nine miles, from Rushton Spencer to Mow Cop. This picturesque and varied walk provides an extension to the *Gritstone Trail* and the *Staffordshire Way*.

The *Biddulph Valley Way* is also an enjoyable circular route which includes the Congleton Edge, The Cloud and Mow Cop.

AROUND WRENBURY

Start: The Cotton Arms (SJ 591 480)

Route: Wrenbury Bridge - Sproston Wood Farm - Shropshire Union Canal (Llangollen Branch) - Starkey's Bridge - Wrenbury Church

Distance: 6 miles

By Car: Take the A49 north from Whitchurch. After crossing the canal, take the second right turn (signposted Wrenbury). Turn left immediately, then stay on this road until it runs beside the canal to a junction. Turn right here and the *Cotton Arms* soon comes into view on the left.

Cotton Arms
Tel: 01270 780377

This pub is named after the local Cotton family, once resident at nearby Combermere Abbey. Its oldest beams were salvaged from ships and a stream runs through the cellar, ensuring that the beer is kept cool at all times.

The variety and quality of reasonably priced, home-made meals cater for vegetarians and traditional eaters, and include seafood, salads and spicy fare. The food is also highly recommended by the locals.

Walk this way ...

Leave the carpark and turn right.

The Dusty Miller was originally a grain mill. Powered by a side wheel, it used water from the River Weaver as it passes in a culvert under the canal here. Later, the building became a warehouse for

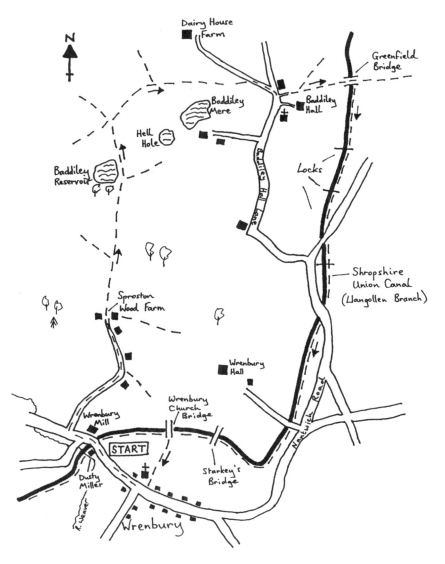

goods taken down the canal in 'fly boats' to market in Manchester, including locally produced Cheshire cheese. It was converted into a country inn in 1977.

Continue across the wooden bascule (lift) bridge.

Raised and lowered by counterbalancing beam weights, it is believed to be one of only two of its type in the country to carry road traffic. Beside it stands Wrenbury Mill, now a boatyard and well stocked craft shop.

Take the first right turn along a pot-holed lane and continue down it all the way to Sproston Wood Farm. Keep ahead past barns, byres and farm buildings, then go through a grey, steel gate at the far end.

Keep ahead on a track, with the hedge on your left, looking for a stile part-way along it. Climb over this and continue ahead with the hedge now on your right, passing a huge sycamore. Continue in the same direction, after negotiating a stile in the electric fence, to a stile at the far end of the field, after a pond.

Keep ahead again, leaving the hedge shortly after a fence jump between two oaks, to make for a stile in the facing hedge. Walk straight over the next field, keeping to the left of oak trees and a silted marlpit until you see a stile.

From here, go ahead again alongside the bank of Baddiley Reservoir to a stile in the facing fence, after which you can walk up the bank for a view of the reservoir. The surrounding trees, bushes and reeds reflect eerily in the still water, only disturbed by ducks a-dipping or the circles of surfacing fish.

Walk uphill across the next field to a stile in the facing fence. Turn right, with the fence on your right, passing above Hell Hole and Baddiley Mere, to a stile. After negotiating both stile and plank bridge out of the next field, turn right to a grey, steel gate.

Cross the huge field here, at first following the line of pylons, then continuing beside the hedge all the way to a gate. In the next field, veer right and go through a large gap in a barbed wire fence, then continue beside this to a copse of elder, ash and hawthorn, behind which is another stile.

Keep ahead again, along the fence to a stile under an ash, then go forward by the hedge until you eventually spot a stile which leads to the drive of Dairy House Farm. Turn right here and, at its end, turn right again. After passing Baddiley Hall Farm and a pond with waterlilies you soon reach Baddiley Church, in its idyllic setting.

*Dedicated to St Michael, **Baddiley Church** has an ancient wooden bellcote and the western gable dates back to 1308, when the building was timber-framed with plaster infilling. Brick eventually replaced the plaster and a brick nave was added in 1811. Its roof, however, is still medieval, as also is the timberwork in the chancel. Inside, a Georgian west gallery overlooks the old box pews and there's a rare little three-decker pulpit.*

***Baddiley Hall**, a tall, timbered building hidden in trees, was originally the home of the Mainwaring family, wealthy Cheshire landowners.*

Retrace your steps almost to the farm, then turn right down a cart-track. Walk straight over the facing field, cross the canal on Greenfield Bridge, then drop down onto the towpath, turning left under the bridge. Continue past three locks and under several bridges.

The Shropshire Union Canal was built by Thomas Telford around 1790 to carry lime, grain and local produce. This is the Llangollen Branch which diverts into Wales from the main canal at nearby Hurleston. The stretch around Wrenbury is characterised by its single-span, timber, bascule bridges.

At bridge number 17 you pass a pretty beech copse. Take care along this section as the towpath almost runs into the canal. Keep ahead again at Starkey's Bridge — named after the local squires, who had a stork as their coat-of-arms.

At Wrenbury Church Bridge, another authentic bascule bridge now beautifully restored, turn left over a stile and leave the canal behind. Walk along the side of the field with the hedge on your right, then cross the next field to a kissing gate into the churchyard.

*Erected on the site of a 12th century chapel, **St Margaret's Church** dates from around 1500 and is dedicated to St Margaret of Antioch, patron saint of expectant mothers. The red sandstone for its construction was brought by cart from quarries on the Bickerton Hills, eight miles away.*

The church's most unusual feature is the whipper's pew just inside the door. Here the dog whipper sat in a blue gown, with yellow tippet and long, white rod. His duty was to evict dogs who barked or fought during a service and also, perhaps, to waken those worshippers who dozed off during a lengthy sermon. In 1826 his title was changed to Beadle — a character featured in Punch and Judy shows.

After visiting the church, which is kept open, leave by the main gates and you are facing the large, picturesque village green. Once a common for grazing livestock, today it provides a central location for May Queen celebrations and the church's summer fete.

Opposite stands Elm House, a timber-framed dwelling dating from the 17th century. To your left is the village store and post office, on the far side of which stands Hawk House, an 18th century building once used as a public house.

To finish the walk, turn right along Cholmondeley Road, back to a warm welcome at the *Cotton Arms*.

EAST CHESHIRE

Alderley Edge   *The Wizard*

Incorporating several wild woodlands and fields planted with a variety of crops, this gently undulating route also provides some surprising views of the adjacent countryside and, even on a Bank Holiday will take you 'far from the madding crowd'.

Gawsworth Common   *Fools Nook*

On a chilly day this walk will soon have you warm. The first hour is a steady uphill climb, but it's downhill almost all the way after that!

Mobberley Brook   *Plough & Flail*

With an outward journey over fields and streams, the return route traverses the infamous Lindow Moss where an Iron Age man and woman were discovered in the 1980s, perfectly preserved by the peat.

Swettenham   *Swettenham Arms*

On this walk you will see many varieties of venerable English trees, some in parkland, others once planted in orchards and gardens. The route follows the looping River Dane and there's a fine view of Stephenson's 23-arched Twemlow Viaduct.

The Peovers   *Bells of Peover*

This delightful stroll winds along beside a pretty stream, takes in two ancient churches and a mellow hall set in gardens well worth a visit.

Found on the wall in the Fool's Nook at Oakgrove ...

A publican stood at the golden gate
His head was bent and low
He meekly asked the man at the gate
Which way was he to go.
"What did you do on earth," asked St Peter,
"To seek admission here?"
"I kept a public house," he said
"For many and many a year."
St Peter opened wide the gate
And then he rang the bell.
"Come inside and choose your harp
You've had your share of hell!"

AROUND ALDERLEY EDGE

Start: The Wizard (SJ 859 773)

Route: Artists Lane - Bradford Lane - Finlow Hill Wood - (Hare Hill) - Alder Wood - Oak Road - Daniel Hill - Waterfall Wood - The Edge.

Distance: 5 miles

By Car: Take the B5087 south-east from Alderley Edge village. After passing *The Wizard*, turn left into the free National Trust carpark, which has toilets. (In a stable behind *The Wizard* is an exhibition of *The Edge*'s history and folklore.)

The Wizard

Tel: 01625 584000

The Wizard is really a restaurant, to have a drink you have to eat and there's no beer. However, walkers are welcome, the food's all home-made and even the soup and sandwiches are superbly different. You might fancy Mexican bean soup with tortillas and soured cream, or ciabatta filled with roast lamb and balsamic shallots. The sweets are mouth-watering too, how about trying blackberry crème brûlée with shortbread, chocolate and orange torte or iced cherry parfait. So treat yourselves and enjoy! (*The Wizard* is shut on a Monday.)

Walk this way ...

From the carpark, walk to the main road and turn right, then immediately left opposite *The Wizard,* down the road signposted to Nether Alderley and Chelford.

This is aptly named Artists Lane which, with its magnificent beeches and rural nature, must indeed be a veritable delight to paint.

To avoid the spasmodic traffic, take the unmarked path atop the left bank just before a lay-by and walk on this all the way down to a bend sign. Return to the road and, after passing *Topps Farm,* turn left along a sometimes muddy footpath, which crosses a stream, then continues to a stile (complete with dog panel) into a field.

Follow trees, then a hedge on your left, and walk under power lines before crossing the line of an old fence to reach a stile under an oak. Continue between trimmed hedges, then turn left along cobble-stoned Bradford Lane, passing a cottage and Bradford Hall Farm

You will soon see a waymark and a public path in the trees on your right. Climb over the stile beside a gate, then keep left along the fence to another waymarked stile. After this walk up a rough and rising meadow to another stile, then continue up the next field (between its two levels) veering slightly right to a sturdy stile, under a fir. Keep forward alongside the wood here to two stiles at its far end.

Why two? As the parish boundary runs between them it might be non-co-operation between local councils, or just an oversight!

Keep ahead again, up and over the next field, beside a line of native trees, then a hedge, to a stile in the far corner. Turn left along a fence to a stile, then continue down the track away from Finlow Hill Farm.

There is plenty to see on the horizon here — Croker Hill with its array of aerials, Shutlingslow's triangular peak and the wooded slopes of Macclesfield Forest.

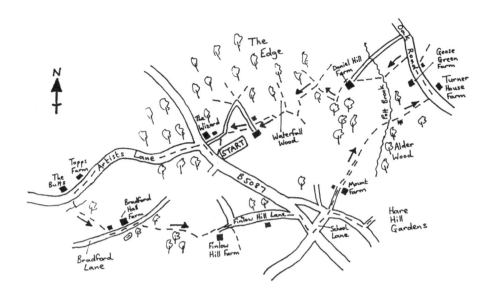

Join Finlow Hill Lane on a bend and keep ahead to walk alongside Finlow Hill Wood. You soon pass stables on the right, which offer riding for handicapped people, before the road curves to reach the busy B5087. Turn right and walk on the horse track beside the road to a crossroads. From here, turn left towards Prestbury, noticing the red 'phone box as you set off down School Lane.

As you pass the sadly derelict village primary school the partially roofless outside loos are plainly visible at each end of the playground.

Soon afterwards you arrive at a junction.

For a short detour to visit Hare Hill Gardens turn right, walking on the footpath beside the parkland wall to the entrance.

Hare Hill is a National Trust property and there is an entrance fee. Allow one to two hours for the visit, which is most rewarding in May and June when the rhododendrons and azaleas are at their best.

Leaving Hare Hill follow the green-arrowed, clearly marked concessionary path until you rejoin the walk at *.

If not including Hare Hill ...

From the junction take the farm track straight ahead down to Mount Farm. Continue between the red brick house and an attractive barn with patterned bricks and cockerel weather vane, then go through a small, steel gate onto a churned-up cow-track. Go over the next stile by a green gate, after which the track rises and becomes drier.

Continue over the field to a stile. Here, ignore the path to Hare Hill and keep ahead along the edge of Alder Wood, following it round to the right and into a dip. Negotiate the stile here, ignoring the one on your right and bear left uphill.

* The Hare Hill detour rejoins the route in this field.

Keep left over the meadow to a stile under oaks in the hedge at the end of the first woodland. Walk up the next field towards Turner House Farm, go through the gate and turn left along Oak Road. After passing Goose Green Farm turn left over a stile in the hedge under two trees.

Keep ahead alongside the hedge and over field stiles. Three fishing ponds can be seen over to the right as you continue down to the footbridge over Pott Brook, which trickles along through the wood.

Turn left up the bank to a field stile, then continue, with the hedge on your left, to a stile by a dilapidated gate. Cross the following field, aiming for the right-hand end of Daniel Hill Farm. Walk beside the wall here, then cross the farm track and the stile opposite.

In this field, at first bear left alongside the house, then climb up the steep slope (muddy at the top) to reach a wood. Negotiate a stile here and turn right along a wire fence, which rises to a junction of paths.

At the base of stone steps, topped by the Hare Hill estate sign, turn right over a stone stile, then drop down the bank and pass through a small, slot gate marked *The Edge*. From here, climb up steps to a narrow path between bracken.

You may perhaps sit on one of the two rustic seats along here to enjoy the view of Woodford Aerodrome. Then, on entering a wood, negotiate the stile on your left. In the field, walk ahead alongside the right-hand fence and turn left along the top hedge to another stile, which leads along a narrow path between wires to a new stile.

Turning right over the stile here takes you on a short detour into the wood, to see a pretty waterfall — but don't expect Niagara!

Retrace your steps and keep straight on up the muddy track, over a stile then right along a wire fence to another stile. From here, turn left uphill, passing a dead tree on the way to a stile, then a track. Go through the narrow entrance ahead, waymarked to the carpark, and cross fields between wires before bearing left down a stony track.

Stay on this for an ice cream, a cup of tea, or some other welcome refreshment at *The Wizard*. However, to go straight back to your car, on your left there's a gap by a gate at the wood's end, which takes you diagonally across the field to a hedge gap into the carpark.

After refreshment you may enjoy a short walk to explore the delights of *The Edge*.

Alderley Edge provides some superb scenery, pleasant strolls, intriguing history and magical legends. Today, many of the views have been obscured by trees — giant beech, Scots pine, sweet chestnut, oak and larch — but Stormy Point provides one outlook.

The Hermit's Garden, found in a quarry behind the Wizard Inn, is my favourite spot. Originally created by Evans, a qualified architect who abandoned the rat-race to live here in peaceful seclusion, he taught the local children much about country lore. However, one day a lad drank from a bottle of bleach believing it to be lemonade and, although acquitted of murder, he was unable to face the horror and committed suicide. Today, his cabin's foundations and cobbled patio form a feature of this peaceful, landscaped area.

AROUND GAWSWORTH COMMON

Start: Fool's Nook (SJ 917 694)

Route: Radcliffe Road - Croker Hill - Bosley Reservoir - Stonyfold
         - Macclesfield Canal - Oakgrove

Distance: 7 miles

By Car: Take the A523 south from Macclesfield. *Fool's Nook* is
         on the left at Oakgrove, on a bad bend where the road to
         Gawsworth goes off to the right across the canal bridge.

Fool's Nook
Tel: 01260 252254

This early 19th century pub in the tiny hamlet of Oakgrove, although
first named the *Royal Oak*, has been known locally as *The Nook* for
much of its history and was officially renamed *Fool's Nook* in 1962.
Two intriguing explanations have been put forward for the origin of
this name. The first is that *nook* is an old English word for bend and
the pub stands on one so severe that many a driver has ended up in the
canal. The second is that jesters, plying their trade on the large local
estates, such as Gawsworth or the Harrington estate at Bosley, used
to meet at the pub for a drink.

A fine selection of Real Ale is on offer, including Boddington's, as
well as a choice of wine and over fifty whiskies. The menu changes
regularly. Most dishes are home-made using fresh ingredients, and
the 'specials' are popular. Food is available every day from noon until
2.30pm and in the evening. The inn is open all day on Sunday and is
closed on Monday in Winter.

Antique furniture and bright brassware add to the character of the
rooms and the pleasant back garden is a quiet place in which to relax

on warm, sunny days. Walking groups are always welcome at this friendly, attractive inn — noted for the quality of its food and beer. As a notice says: 'We don't serve fast food. We serve good food as fast as we can.'

Walk this way ...

From the carpark turn left up Radcliffe Road, perhaps accompanied by a joyous miscellany of birdsong as you trudge uphill. At the entrance to Hawkshead Quarry veer left along Leek Old Road, then take the next right turn up Croker Lane — a No Through Road.

As you climb steadily higher the massive aerial materialises ahead on Croker Hill and the saucer-shaped satellite at Jodrell Bank rises unrealistically above the plain. At Lee Hills Quarry keep ahead between pillars, perhaps accompanied by a softly shining sun — or maybe not!

The drive to Croker House Kennels bears off on your right and you continue over a cattle grid, then past rough-hewn, sandstone monoliths, symbolic of this heavily quarried area, on the way to Croker Farm. Stay on the track here, negotiating another cattle grid and continuing to Hanging Gate Farm.

Turning left up the track here, the view over Gawsworth Quarry and Common begins to unfold as you climb ever higher. Eventually, you leave the track where it bears right and negotiate a facing stile, then turn right and follow the Gritstone Trail along the wall.

Here, the view over the other side of the ridge runs from Macclesfield Forest in the north, to the slopes around Wildboarclough, dominated by Shutlingsloe's distinctive outline.

You climb steadily until you pass through a steel gate, cross a stile and are confronted by the monstrous aerial. From here, keep ahead for a short distance along the track of loose, white stones until you reach a junction in front of the mast and turn right downhill, leaving the Gritstone Trail. (It's downhill almost all the way from here!)

Bosley Cloud is prominent to the left, backed by the Mow Cop ridge, and below lie the tranquil waters of Bosley Reservoir.

Stay on this track, passing through a kissing gate, then turn right through a black gate as you reach the byres of Upton Fold Farm. Follow the hawthorn hedge down from here and turn left over a stile beside an ash.

Walk to the end of the short fence on your right, then keep in the same direction over the field to a cart-track. Bear right on it, winding down the hill until you see a stile under holly trees, up to your left in a facing fence. Cross the gully here, via a substantial wooden bridge.

Next, drop down the sloping field into the valley and join another cart-track which rises to a stile. After this, continue along the deeply rutted, sometimes messy cow-track, bordered by hawthorn, holly, oak and ash, all the way to a barn.

Cross a facing stile and continue forward with the hedge on your right. After passing a pond the track materialises again and continues all the way down to the A54, where you turn right. Take great care as you round the corner.

Covering 20 acres, Bosley Reservoir was constructed in 1832 to feed water into the Macclesfield Canal. Reeds and trees are mirrored in this large expanse of water, which certainly enhances the landscape.

Turn right up Brooks Lane and, after passing a black-doored building, turn left over a stile and walk up the field to the end of an obsolete hawthorn hedge. Keep it on your left until you drop down to a stile, then follow the field boundary in the same direction all the way to Hollins Farm.

You can see much of your earlier route from here.

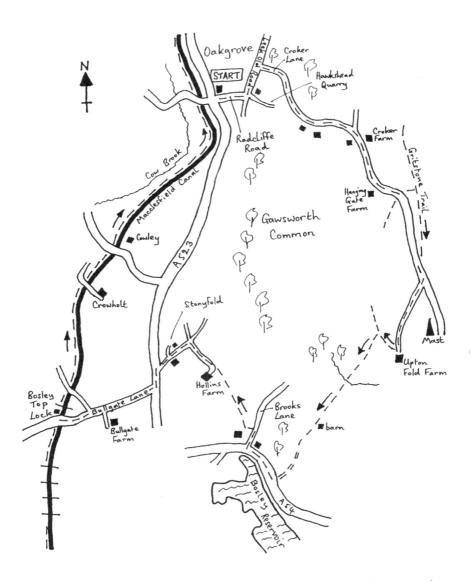

Turn right along a rough road, then left at a junction, passing Stonyfold on your way down to the main road. Turn left here and immediately right down Bullgate Lane, towards North Rode.

Looking at the cumulus shape of The Cloud from here you can see just how it got its name.

You soon pass Bullgate Farm, with its attractive garden, then turn right along the canal towpath at Bosley Top Lock. Don't panic when a sandstone milestone indicates that it's 16 miles to Marple, you aren't walking that far!

Thomas Telford designed this extraordinary waterway, which seems to ignore the land's contours. Opened in 1832 it was one of the last canals to be built before trains superseded canal boats. Between here and the aqueduct near Bosley, twelve locks raise the canal 110 feet in only a mile and, used almost exclusively for leisure now, this canal forms part of the Cheshire Ring, joining up with the Bridgewater Canal, and the Trent & Mersey, to encircle much of the county.

As you walk north, elderberry bushes line the bank, in early Autumn their branches bent almost double by bunches of blue-black berries. Delightful stone bridges span the canal around Crowholt and Cowley, and Cow Brook threads its way over fertile meadows beneath banks of gorse. Finally, journey's end is in sight as you cross a swing bridge, then the busy road, with care, back to the *Fool's Nook* and some welcome refreshment.

AROUND MOBBERLEY BROOK

Start: Plough and Flail (SJ 817 798)

Route: Paddock Hill - Moss Farm - B5085 - Noah's Ark - Wilmslow Golf Course - Merryman's Lane - Chorley Old Hall - Carr Lane - Row-of-Trees - Lindow Moss

Distance: 6.5 miles

By Car: Take the B5085 from Knutsford towards Alderley Edge. From Mobberley, continue to Knolls Green and take the next left turn (down Moss Lane) **after** the *Bird in Hand* pub. Bear right onto Paddock Hill Lane, then left for the *Plough and Flail.*

Plough and Flail

Tel: 01565 873537

Hidden away on the edge of the peat bog where the famous Lindow Pete was found, the *Plough and Flail* was once four cottages inhabited by farm workers. In the 1860s, the tenant in the end cottage started to brew his own beer, which he sold to other farm workers, and eventually this cottage became the 'local'. It also gained a reputation as a meeting place for poachers and a press report early in the 20th century described it as, 'a public house which gives way to much disorder and frequent fights' — a far cry from its reputation today.

The name of the inn reflects a bygone age, when a shire horse pulled a plough to prepare fields for crops and a flail was used to separate grain from chaff. Both were important farm implements in the 19th century. Supposedly, there's a friendly ghost — an old gentleman in black cap and gaiters, who sits in the inglenook fireplace holding out spectral hands to the blaze.

W R Bates, the renowned rugby player, was landlord here in the 1970s. The Cooper family from Lower Peover, who developed the company, *Freshbake Foods*, then owned the *Plough and Flail* for several years, when the landlord-cum-chef was Julian Laffan. Of French, Irish and Belgian extraction (what you might call a European mongrel!) he believed in serving fresh food made on the premises at realistic prices — a practice which still continues today with the inn's imaginative and extensive menu.

Originally converted from a wash-house and barn in 1978, the restaurant area, now known as *The Cottage,* is no smoking, and the sunny conservatory is an attractive, recent addition. The bar, with its exposed brickwork, old oak beams and log fire, serves *Real Ale* (*Boddies* and *Pedigree* are always on offer) and wines are a speciality.

Outside, the garden's fruit trees provide apples in season, when delicious apple and cheese pies enhance the already tempting array of sweets. Vegetarians are well catered for too, with dishes which can be specially prepared to a person's taste using fresh produce. Families with children are asked to use the snug, and outside, in addition to a sandpit and climbing frame, there's also plenty of room for football.

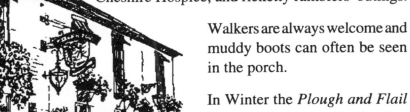

The Cheshire 'drag' hunt often visits the pub and other events are ladies' lunches supporting the East Cheshire Hospice, and ricketty ramblers' outings.

Walkers are always welcome and muddy boots can often be seen in the porch.

In Winter the *Plough and Flail* is open all day on Sunday but from noon to 3pm and from 6pm in the evenings during the rest of the week. However, in Summer it's open all day, every day.

Walk this way ...

Leave the carpark and turn right and right again over a stile, which takes you along a field footpath to a sloping stile in the fence ahead. Bear left along the hedge here to another stile, then keep ahead over the next field to a further stile by a willow. After this, follow the fence to another stile and walk forward, passing through a small gate before bearing left down a country lane past Moss Farm.

Stay on this lane until you bear right at a junction, then go left over a stile as you round a bend after Greenacres and Moss Cottage. Next, keep ahead alongside a wooden fence to another stile, from which you continue in the same direction, negotiating stiles until you walk down the drive beside Bluebell Cottage to the busy B5085.

Cross over with care and turn left. After passing Brown House Farm, both scarp and dip slopes of Alderley Edge can be seen in sharp relief as you turn right over a stile opposite a pair of semi-detached houses. Cross the field diagonally left, following the dip caused by an underground stream, then continuing along the hedge to a stile. From here, drop down to cross Whim Brook and climb up the next field, beside oak trees at first, then ahead to a tatty stile onto a country lane.

Turn right here and, after crossing Mobberley Brook, turn left up the drive to Noah Wood House, continuing over stiles and past the substantial barn known as Noah's Ark. Cross a small field to another stile, then keep ahead beside the fence until you turn left at a stile onto a rough, grassy track. Pass a reed-fringed pool before Springfield Farm, then keep forward down the farm road.

Turn right down Warford Lane, then go left over a stile in the middle of a copse. From here you cross the golf course. Daunting though this may seem, make for the left-hand end of a silver birch copse, then to a stile in the fence behind hole 15. From here, turn right round the field's edge to a stile, then turn right again and keep forward to Merryman's Lane by the private nursing home of Abberley House.

Turn left here, then cross the main road from Alderley to Chelford (A535), with care, and go over the facing stile. Bear diagonally left across the field, passing two oaks, to reach a stile in the far corner. Cross the track here and walk straight across the next field to another corner stile. Keep ahead, passing a fishing pool, to reach a bridge over a stream, then walk forward beside the fence until you turn right over another bridge in the far corner.

From here, the tall spires of the Alderley churches stand out from a hillside, bedecked by palatial property.

Continue with the hedge on your left all the way to a final stile by extensive glasshouses. Follow the hedge round here, ignoring all stiles until you exit at a bungalow, down a snicket bordered by leylandii and hawthorn. Keep ahead along the rough road here until you eventually fork left onto Green Lane, then turn left into Chorley Hall Lane and left again at the A535.

Along here stands Chorley Old Hall. This superb, black-and-white building of 14th century origin has a moat dug two centuries later to deter opportunist robbers.

After passing the hall climb over a stile on the right. Follow the stream until it disappears underground, then continue along the fence until you turn right along a stony track to a stile by a gate. From here, walk through the farmyard of Common Carr Farm before veering left to a stile. Next, keep beside the hedge along a grassy track to another stile and go down a gravel drive to Carr Lane. Continue forward past sewage works to reach the B5085 at the area known as Row-of-Trees.

Cross over with care and turn right for a short way before going left down a stony track between Cottage Farm and Cloud Cottage — the end one of a terrace. Keep ahead over stiles to cross Lindow peat bog, the soft, sheltered, black path winding eerily between stunted trees.

It is hard to imagine that peat cutting was once a thriving industry in this now-deserted area.

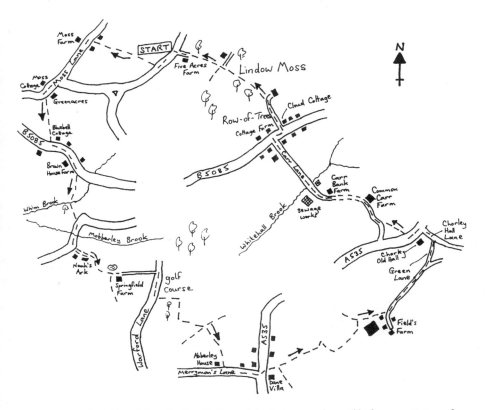

Cross a field beside a belt of silver birch to reach a stile by a gate made of fence posts. Then keep ahead again, passing a farm on a track to reach a bridge over a ditch. Continue in the same direction across a field, with journey's end at last in sight. The route continues over stiles separated by ponds, then behind the stables of Five Acres Farm to the road, where a final left turn takes you back for some well-earned refreshment at the *Plough and Flail*.

AROUND SWETTENHAM

Start: Swettenham Arms (SJ 800 672)

Route: Swettenham Lane - Daffodil Dell - Cross Lane - A535 (Twemlow Viaduct) - Woodhouse Farm - River Dane - Swettenham Church

Distance: 7 miles

By Car: Travelling on the A34 north from Congleton, take the second left turn (to Swettenham). Go left at a junction and immediately right into Messuage Lane. Keep ahead at crossroads and straight on until you turn left onto Congleton Road. Cross the brook and turn right into Swettenham Lane. The inn is then on the right after the church.

Swettenham Arms

Tel: 01477 571284

Tucked away behind the parish church, the Swettenham Arms is found down a road which only leads to this tranquil village in the Dane Valley. Emerging from the dark and daunting conifers which surround its large carpark you come face-to-face with this unspoilt, pre-17th century, country inn.

Part of the building, which was once a nunnery, may date back to the 13th century and it was the custom for funeral parties travelling some distance, to stay overnight with the body at the nunnery — a welcome resting place for the weary even then! Next morning the coffin was taken to church via an underground passage, blocked up long ago.

Meals are served seven days a week, lunchtimes and evenings. Parties of walkers are very welcome but are asked to book first and then remove their boots at the door!

Cask-conditioned Real Ale includes Greenalls Original, Tetley's and Jennings' Bitter. Addlestone's cask conditioned cider is also on tap. All the food is home-made, freshly cooked on the premises each day and there's plenty of choice and originality.

Inside, ancient, oak beams enhance the decor, together with real coal fires in Winter. In Summer the tables on the terrace outside are well used and at all times you can be sure of a homely, happy atmosphere.

Walk this way ...

Leave the pub carpark, turn left along Swettenham Lane towards the church and go immediately right over a stile and along a snicket between gardens. Cross the facing field, pass to the right of two ancient limes and, with the hedge on your left, walk to a stile and gate by a sycamore.

Stay in the same direction, alongside the fence to another stile — this time under an oak. Go ahead again to a stile and another sycamore, and from the copse here, strike out across the field (bearing slightly left) to another copse and the exit, well to the left of a stately beech.

Walk down to the road on Swettenham Hall's drive. Unless you want a very short walk, do not turn sharp left here into Swettenham Lane, but take the next left turn down Congleton Road, dropping steeply downhill to cross the bridge over Swettenham Brook.

To the right, behind Swettenham Mill, is Daffodil Dell, well worth a springtime visit when it's grassy slopes are covered in golden glory.

Continue uphill, passing the turning back to Swettenham via a ford, then a farm road, then the Kermincham sign at a beck, at which point a footpath sign comes into view. Turn left over a stile here and walk along the fence on your right, passing a sturdy bench in it — for hay or milk churns perhaps. Then, after passing a small stable, turn right over a stile under the second oak.

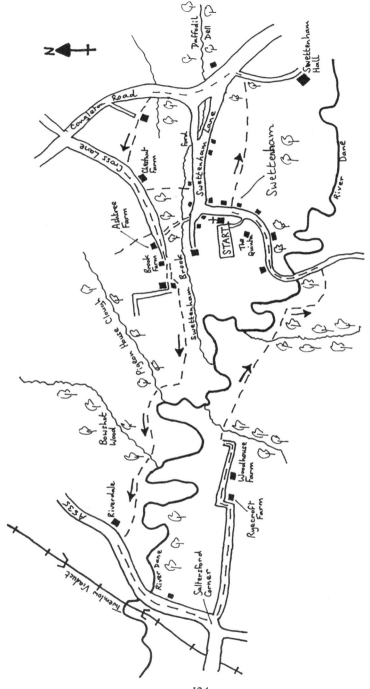

Continue in the same direction, but with the fence on your left and notice the jump in it. Pass an attractive farmhouse complex to reach a stile onto the drive, which you cross, then continue behind a barn to another stile. Stay in the same direction along the field's edge, noticing the sign, 'Landowners welcome caring walkers.' Hopefully, all readers of this are also appreciative of caring landowners!

Pass an oak, once probably the end of a hedge, and continue to a corner stile, hidden under a holly. From here, bear left along Cross Lane, passing the Swettenham Meadows Nature Reserve, then Chestnut Farm with its ancient barn.

A left turn over a stile along here is another shortcut, this time down into the valley and back up to Swettenham.

However, for the full walk, continue beside a lovely, natural woodland, at the end of which, opposite Ashtree Farm, a sharp left turn also returns to the walk's start. (That's your last chance!)

Keep ahead through a blue gate, then along a green lane to Brook Farm. Pass this, and an old, white-painted water pump, before turning left over a stile before a brick barn. Walk behind this to another stile, then keep forward and along a path between bracken and hedgerows.

Walk along the top of a grassy bank beside the hedge, to a stile by a gate. Continue forward beside a belt of bracken to a stile between oak and elder. Keep along the right-hand edge of the next field, passing a sunny pond, fringed by bullrushes, on the way to a stile.

From here, walk straight across the field, with a fence on your left, then drop downhill, to cross a clear stream and pass through a gate into an enchanting woodland. Bear left uphill past crab apples, and exit by a stile at the top.

From here you have a glimpse of the giant telescope at Jodrell Bank.

Turn left along the field's side and keep left through a gateway — or over a stile with many nettles! Drop down the side of the next field, until you turn right at an area of rough ground dividing fields. Walk along the top edge of this and continue with a band of firs on your left. At the end, drop down through grass, then into a woodland strip via stile or gate. Continue down through this, exiting by a small gate.

Walk across the next field, eventually continuing along its left side with the River Dane murmuring below, and perhaps even glinting in the sun! Keep ahead at a stile, with the hedge on your right and a view of Twemlow Viaduct. The stile onto the busy A535 is then in the hedge ahead after you pass the house, *Riverdale*.

Twemlow Viaduct, the largest on the Manchester-Crewe railway line, is one of Robert Stephenson's most splendid feats of engineering. Completed in 1841, each symmetrical bow of its 23 arches soars in a 63-foot span high above the flat, valley floor.

Turn left and take great care as you continue on the left-hand side of the road, to the start of a footpath. The road then crosses the River Dane on an old stone bridge, passes Saltersford Cottage and rises to Saltersford Corner. Here, it's a great relief to turn left into the quiet serenity of the road to Woodhouse Farm, hemmed in with hawthorn.

The road bears left to pass in front of Ryecroft Farm, then right and on again, with another view of Jodrell Bank's telescope. Myriads of red admiral butterflies may be fluttering busily amongst the buddleia which border the track as you continue, with wonderful views over to Shutlingsloe and Bosley Cloud.

Rabbits scamper for cover in the sandy soil as the cart-track drops downhill and ends at a stile. Veer right immediately, over a rickety stile into a wood. Walk down a tiny path, cross a stream and negotiate another stile.

Cross this large field, making for the end of a hedge on the left, where there's a broken stile. Keep ahead again for a short distance, with the River Dane below, then drop steeply down the hillside under an oak and bear right in the lee of the bank.

At a wooden gate continue along the valley floor, by the placid stream at first then along the wood's side, squelching through a very wet water meadow until you can go no farther and turn right over a stile above the tortuously meandering river. Climb up through the wood — a steep pull — and turn left at the top to walk alongside a field.

From here there's a lovely view of the river, spanned by an attractive bridge, and your earlier route is visible along the valley's far side.

The tiny path winds up and down through the wood, until steps lead down to a gate. Turn left along the gravel bridleway here, through a horse gate and over the green bridge seen from above. Horse chestnut and ash shade the track at the wood's edge as you come to a white gate, then rosehips and redcurrants abound in the hedgerow as the lane winds uphill and into Swettenham.

Note the sympathetically converted old parish school opposite The Quinta's entrance.

St Peter's Church

A Saxon cross found in the south aisle signifies a church here way back in time. The timber framework we see today, however, dates back to the 13th century and was encased in brick in 1720. The church's several roofs are covered in heavy, grey flags and the chancel has curious, oval windows.

The yew trees on the east side of the church are of great age and are first mentioned in the parish records of 1663, which also include several antidotes to the bite of a mad dog!

Some epitaphs in the graveyard are worth finding, such as —

> *My glass is run, my grave you see,*
> *Wait but a while, you'll follow me.*

And on the grave of Robert Blincoe, Rector here from 1869 to '79, is a sundial which records the latitude of its position — 53° 20'.

AROUND THE PEOVERS

Start: The Bells of Peover (SJ 743 742)

Route: St Oswald's Church - Peover Eye - Long Lane - Peover Hall - Hillcrest House - Windrush - Lower Peover

Distance: 6 miles

By Car: Take the A50 south from Knutsford. Bear right onto the B5081, then take the second left turn in 1.5 miles (where the Plumley turn goes right). After this, the first right turn will take you to the *Bells of Peover.*

Bells of Peover
Tel: 01565 722269

This tiny hamlet with its school, church and pub so close together caused one Vicar to comment that it provided Education, Salvation and Damnation all within a stone's throw of one another! Certainly, George Bell, who combined being landlord of the pub and sexton of the church for many years, would have enjoyed the joke. Today, the old school, dating from the 17th century, is a beautifully-maintained cottage, but the school bell still hangs aloft to signify its origin, and a private nursery school thrives on the premises.

The original building on the pub's site was a priest's house, which then became a hospice where monks and other travellers could spend the night. The present inn, believed to date from 1569, was originally called *The Swan's Neck.* Its name was then changed to the *Warren de Tabley Arms* by landlord, George Bell, who, together with his wife, ran the pub for fifty years.

She came from the *Bird in Hand* at Mobberley and brought with her a recipe for the brewing of beer. It was made where the stables now stand and the building is still known locally as *The Brewery*. The beer was put in stone jars, some of which can still be seen in the pub today. It was then transported by horse and cart and, at that time, the licensee also acted as a wine and spirit merchant for the surrounding area.

The Bells died within five days of each other in 1898 and the pub is now named after them. It is fitting that their grand-daughter runs it so efficiently today and it attracts many visitors from both far and near. Americans particularly enjoy its very Englishness and visiting bell ringers, whose hobby is thirsty work, find it particularly convenient!

All the food is home-made, from steak and kidney pie to beef in red wine, or the specially concocted quiche. And the sweets, produced daily, may include lemon soufflé and raspberry pavlova. Real Ale is served from old-fashioned hand-pumps and the wide selection of wines and other drinks will also titivate your taste buds.

This idyllic inn nestles comfortably in its picturesque setting. The leafy tendrils and delicate flowers of mauve wisteria, which have wound around its doorway for over 150 years, add idyllic charm to the twittering birds and sonorous chimes of the church clock.

St Oswald's Church

Gabled and half-timbered, with a stone tower built later, St Oswald's Church dates from the 14th century. Inside is a Jacobean pulpit and the original box pews. A massive oak chest has a lid so heavy that any girl able to lift it would make a suitable farmer's wife — or so it's said!

The tower houses a ground floor ring of six bells and has an unusual rhyme on the wall. In the graveyard, there's a striking monument to the well known poet and naturalist, Lord de Tabley, whose specialist subjects were brambles and spiders.

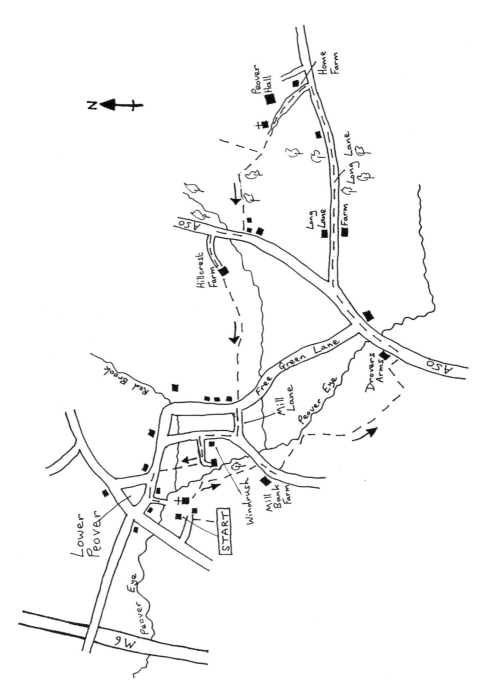

N

Peover Hall
Home Farm
Long Lane
Long Lane
Farm
A50
Hillcrest Farm
Red Brook
Free Green Lane
Mill Lane
Peover Eye
Drovers Arms
A50
Lower Peover
Peover Eye
Windrush
Mill Bank Farm
START
M6

Walk this way ...

Leave the churchyard via an oak kissing gate in the far right-hand corner. Follow the grassy track slightly to the right across the field and drop down to a pretty stream — the Peover Eye. Keeping this, and the trees, on your left walk forward to a country lane. Cross a stile in the facing hedge and follow a narrow, waymarked path.

Cross undulating fields, following waymarks and a line of stiles, then walk on a path to a further stile, ignoring a gate on the right. Finally, walk along the hedge and turn left onto the A50, perhaps pausing at *The Drovers Arms*, which dates from 1842 and has proper coffee!

Continue along the road, crossing the Peover Eye and passing the sign for Peover Superior, then cross to the other pavement and turn right down Long Lane. Walk through a coppice of beech and oak and pass Saint Anthony's houses with their oak-beamed eaves.

The giant telescope of Jodrell Bank sweeps the skies nearby and, in the distance, Bosley Cloud rears above the Pennine foothills.

Turn sharp left at the signpost to the church and the sweet smell of hay and freshly-sawn logs may greet you as you pass the stables and the high doors to the haylofts.

Imagine how the hay would once have been pitchforked into these lofts from a farm cart, then spread out to dry on the warm floor, the steaming breath from horses stabled below rising to aid the process.

Bear right and left, passing more 17th century stables.

Inside is carved, Jacobean woodwork and ornamental plaster ceilings, and the tower is now topped by an ornate weather vane mounted on a golden ball.

Continue to the gardens, which date from Tudor times and are open to the public on Monday afternoons — an honesty box placed trustingly for visitors' fees.

A great cedar shades the lawns sweeping up to Over Peover Hall. This Elizabethan mansion replaced an older, timber building in the 16th century and its gables reach high above mullioned windows, which peep out from the mellow brick walls. It was occupied by the American General 'Old Blood and Guts' Patton during the 2nd World War, when his British headquarters was in Knutsford.

'With speedy foot the age goes by,' are the words faintly engraved on the 17th century sundial on the way to the church of St Lawrence.

Inside, wooden pillars support a superb hammerbeam roof. There are many monuments to the Mainwaring family and the American flag was presented to the church after victory in the 2nd World War.

Continue through a dark arcade of yews as the grounds sweep away in peaceful magnificence. Then admire a massive oak, a riot of rhododendrons and a giant beech, before climbing over a stone stile and almost immediately turning left to negotiate another. Then turn slightly right and continue with trees on your left to the house named *Tree Tops* and the thatched, white-painted *Nixon's Cottage*.

Turn right at the A50, then go left down a farm road to Hillcrest Farm, crossing the cattle grid. Pass through the facing gate (waymarked) and cross the gravel to another gate. Next, keep the hedge on your right, noting a gap in the hedge with an incongruous, free-standing tap. At the field's end bear left before going over a stile by a red-brick house, which stands to the left of a row of houses.

Cross the road here and walk down Mill Lane, almost opposite. Take the next right turn and, after passing the house, *Windrush*, turn left down a farm track. As you reach tennis courts on your left, climb over a stile behind a small, derelict brick building on your right.

Walk along with the hedge on your left, dropping down to cross a stout bridge. After this walk up the field ahead until you exit over a stile. Turn left to pass a post-box, then keep left at two more lanes to arrive back in Lower Peover.

THE PENNINES

Billinge Hill   *The Highwayman*

This walk provides the answer for critics who claim that Cheshire is flat. It's not for the faint hearted as the total, overall ascent is well over 1,000 feet, with corresponding descents. However, the climbing is mostly gradual, with only a few short, steep hills, and the route is particularly scenic.

Bollington   *The Windmill*

This is a walk full of diversity and interest. It includes field paths, the Middlewood Way and the history of Bollington's industrial era.

Disley   *The Ploughboy*

Poor Disley, spread-eagled across the frantic A6 between Stockport and Buxton. Yet Disley is surrounded by an exhilarating landscape of reservoirs, rocky outcrops and rolling vistas, and the Friends Meeting House, on Ring o' Bells Lane, provides an oasis of tranquility.

Lamaload   *The Stanley*

Perhaps the most strenuous walk in the book, the first part, around Lamaload Reservoir, will get you in training for what's to come!

Tegg's Nose   *Leather's Smithy*

Here, there's the choice of a longer or shorter walk. Both take in Macclesfield Forest, views of the reservoirs which supply water to the surrounding area, and the history of quarrying on Tegg's Nose.

Round in Circles

NB These details were correct at the time. Every care has been taken to ensure that this walk embraces at least three folds of the map.

Turn on your heel and leave the carpark.

Follow the path until you reach a drystone wall.

Passing through the wall continue till you reach the third sheep on your right.

Here take a sharp left turn and keep climbing where the grass is green.

As you reach the brow, turn to admire the well-loved contours of You-Should-Know-It Fell behind you.

Continue upwards keeping cloud nine always in view and you will easily reach the well-defined ridge.

Keep ascending through the incipient mist until you reach the summit marked by two or three people taking photographs.

Pause to imbibe the visual headiness of the vista.

Begin your descent by putting one foot in front of the other.

Follow the direction of your shadow, keeping the wind in your face.

Turn sharply with the lumbering shape of You-Must-Surely-Recognise-This-One Crag screed gently in front of you.

Keep to the fainter path ignoring its disappearance.

Continue to where it narrows into a beck, and look for the sign saying, 'Did you remember to lock your car?'

Follow any thieves operating in the area back to the starting point.

Jenny Melmoth
Macclesfield

Hopefully, the instructions given for the routes in this book are somewhat clearer than these!

AROUND BILLINGE HILL

Start: Lay-by behind *The Highwayman* (SJ 965 770)

Route: Four Lane Ends - Ginclough - Rainow - Kerridge Hill - White Nancy - Oakenbank - *Cheshire Hunt Inn* - Gritstone Trail to Brink Farm - Further Harrop Farm - Black Brook - Harrop Fold Farm - Withinlow Farm

Distance: 7.5 miles

By Car: From Macclesfield take the A5002, north-east through Hurdsfield, Rainow and the tiny hamlet of Ginclough. Then take the second turn right, signposted to Saltersford and the Goyt Valley. Park in the lay-by on the right after Paddock Knoll Farm.

The Highwayman

Tel: 01625 573245

300 years old, *The Highwayman* used to be called the *Blacksmith's Arms*, but today each bar is named after offenders. There's Turpin's Bar and Tom King's Snug — a local villain. Although bleakly sited this is a cosy pub, its tiny rooms enhanced by old oak beams (take care if you're tall), gleaming copper and an array of Toby jugs. In Winter, there's even three coal fires by which to warm yourself.

To drink, there's Thwaites' beer, bitter and mild, Guinness and Carlsberg lager. The pub is well-known for its Mexican dishes and a blackboard lists the day's 'specials', which may include chicken burrito and vegetarian enchilada alongside the more traditional home-made, steak and kidney pie and lasagne.

Walk this way ...

From the lay-by walk back to the Macclesfield Road (A5002), cross over, turn left and walk uphill, to the stile on the right. As you bear left to cross the corner of the field to another stile, views of the surrounding hills open up. Drop downhill through the gateway into the next field, then continue in the same direction to negotiate a stepladder, then a stile out of the following field.

Keep ahead again and very slightly left (downhill all the way) to steps over the dry-stone wall ahead. (What a feature of this area!) The Saddle of Kerridge rises ahead, stretching from White Nancy to the tapering descent of its southern slopes.

Over to the right is Rainow Low. This cluster of small farms and cottages, snugly sheltering in the lee of Big Low, once formed a tight-knit, working community but is now mainly residential.

Drop down the next field to clamber over the high wall on wide, stone slabs. Then drop further into the valley, climbing over flat slab steps at the next wall and descending between gorse bushes to cross the mill stream as it drops down from Ginclough.

Climb uphill on the opposite bank, between hawthorn bushes, to steps in the wall on your left. (Further along is the silted up reservoir.) Walk over the field, with the pumping station and wall over to your right, to stone steps in the wall ahead. Keep in the same direction to more steps over a wall, then drop down the next field to a stile in the far left-hand corner. From here, turn left up a snicket to the road and a substantial building — once a thriving Methodist chapel.

Turn right along the footpath to the *Robin Hood* pub, which serves coffee and food. Drop off the main road here, down Stocks Lane, walking in the same direction as before past the Institute, which now houses the local playgroup. Further on is the old Methodist school — now a private house.

Turn right here, into Chapel Lane, and keep left down to fir trees, where you turn right down Sugar Lane — a No Through Road. Along here your path up onto Kerridge is clearly visible. At the sign 'Private Road Access Only' turn left over a stile in the holly hedge. Then keep right down the side of the field, beside the fence, and continue down the next field to a stile at the bottom.

Keep dogs under close control if there are sheep in these fields.

Cross both streams as you bear left to climb steeply up onto Kerridge. The view of Rainow opens out as you ascend and this is the perfect place for a picnic.

At the top turn right over a stone stile in the wall and continue along the top of the ridge all the way to White Nancy.

Visible for miles around, this squat, white-washed structure was erected as a folly by the Gaskell family of nearby Ingersley Hall, to commemorate the Battle of Waterloo, fought in 1815.

Drop down the hillside ahead until you turn right along a track which takes you into the valley of the River Dean. Turn left alongside the river and, in the middle of the factory buildings, turn right along an almost hidden path between flat roofs. Then continue left behind the works and walk up the side of the hill to a stile beside an iron gate.

To the right is Savio House, a religious centre run by the Salesian Order, which originally occupied Shrigley Hall — now a golf and country club.

Cross the field, the drive to Savio House and the next field, passing a stand of trees on your right, then a lone hawthorn, to reach a stile. Take the fenced-in track through a narrow wood and over a stream to arrive at Oakenbank Lane at stone steps over a wall.

From here you follow the Gritstone Trail all the way to Brink Farm.

Turn left along Oakenbank Lane, soon passing the house of the hedgehog lover! Cross the road at Blaze Hill, keep ahead down one side of the triangle and turn right towards Pott Shrigley.

If you are not stopping for refreshment at the *Country Café* ahead, cut the corner off by turning right at the start of the footpath, up steps and over a stile into a field. Bear left diagonally over the field, then continue beside a left-hand wall to exit by a wooden gate. From here, turn right up the lane known as Hedge Row, to the inn.

The Cheshire Hunt Inn is a small, traditional country pub with a highly recommended cuisine. It's particularly well-known for its steaks, bought from a local butcher with his own slaughterhouse in sight across the valley.

Turn left immediately after passing the inn over steps in the wall, then bear right down the field to a stile in the fence. Turn left alongside the wall to another stile in the next fence, then bear diagonally right, following Gritstone Trail signs over the next field until you drop down to the attractive packhorse bridge over Harrop Brook.

Cross this and stones to a stile, then continue uphill by a fence at first, then through a copse of silver birch to a hole in the wall behind holly bushes. Keep the stream on your right for a short way, then cross it and walk diagonally up the slope to a track.

Cross this and make for the corner of the wall on your right below the line of trees. Turn right along the wall, climbing to an iron gate and stone stile. From here turn right, following the wall all the way to a cattle grid.

This northerly section gives sweeping views of the Kerridge ridge, with White Nancy at the Bollington end. Below it is Ingersley Hall, once the home of the Gaskell family whose daughter, Nancy, is reputed to have given the name to the folly.

Cross the cattle grid, then leave the farm track immediately to go through a gap in the wall ahead, then over a stile. Walk forward through the spinney, then veer left alongside the tumbledown wall which faces you. For the best views scramble to the top of the oddly named Andrew's Knob on your left.

Cresting Andrew's Knob reveals Blakestone Moor with its capped lead mine shafts, beyond which is Lyme Park. On a clear day, Jodrell Bank, Woodford Aerodrome and Manchester Airport are also visible on the Cheshire Plain.

Contour round to the left below the hilltop, to an erratic with an arrow on it and an abandoned quarry.

In the 18th, 19th and early part of the 20th century, quarrying in this area was a major part of the local economy, the stone being much in demand for road building and roofing material.

Turn right along a track here, passing a pond on the right, then walking over the rise to reach Brink Farm and Bakestonedale Road.

To the east is Charles Head, overlooking Kettleshulme, and climbers may be seen on Windgather Rocks.

Take care as you turn right; this is no longer a quiet lane. Along here you leave the Gritstone Trail, as it bears off to the left to its terminus in Lyme Park, and climb over the stile opposite to drop down two fields (with the wall on your right) to a step-ladder stile. Then keep forward behind the buildings of Further Harrop Farm to a signpost.

Turn left and walk fairly near the wall on your left to a stile. **Do not climb over this** but turn right, dropping down the field, with the fence

on your left (and a valley on your right edged with hawthorn). Walk through a tumbledown wall at a hawthorn bush and continue to descend to a stile in the next wall. After this turn right to cross the bridge over the burbling brook — or have a paddle!

Climb out of the valley, bearing left to a stile on the hilltop. Continue up the next field with the fence/wall on your right, to a stile by a gate. Keep ahead again, over setts, to pass Harrop Fold Farm on your right. Notice the old well in the wall on your left, then the dilapidated barn, and when the farm road bears left, climb over a step-ladder stile ahead. Walk straight on, with the hedge on your right, cross a stile into the next field and keep ahead again to a stile in the wall.

Cross over the private road to New Hey Farm and climb the stile in the fence opposite. Keep ahead, walking alongside an attractive, newly planted copse at first, then making for the step through the wall ahead. Continue beside the hawthorn hedge and fence on your left to stone steps over the next wall.

Now keep ahead, with the wall on your right, passing Withinlow Farm. Walk through a gateway into the next field and carry straight on up to *The Highwayman* and a well-earned rest.

Feeling refreshed, walk uphill on the main road, turn first left towards Saltersford and the Goyt Valley, and a final climb will loosen the joints as you return to the lay-by.

AROUND BOLLINGTON

Start: Windmill Inn (SJ 924 788)

Route: Ashley Farm - Harrop Green Farm - Middlewood Way - Bollington - Clarke Lane - Dumbah Hollow - Butley Town - Whiteley Green

Distance: 6.5 miles

By Car: Travel on the A523 north from Macclesfield. After the B5358 has gone left to Handforth, take the next right turn down Holehouse Lane (signposted Whiteley Green). After passing through this hamlet, you can't miss *The Windmill* on the right.

The Windmill Inn

Tel: 01625 574222

The Windmill is thought to have taken its name from a cornmill, located just north of nearby Five Ashes cottage, which operated in the latter half of the 19th century, but the building itself dates back to the century before, when it was a farmhouse. Since becoming an inn it has always been a local meeting place, and is also popular with ramblers, and boatmen from the nearby Macclesfield Canal.

This slate-roofed, white house tucked away up a quiet country lane retains its farmhouse feel even today, with its wooden floor and old oak beams. The dining area is strictly no smoking and reproduction antique furniture provides a roomy yet homely atmosphere. There's ample parking space and shrub borders enhance the delightful, four-acre garden where children can play. In Summer an outside bar operates, barbecues take place, and a marquee can be hired for that really special occasion.

The Windmill Inn is in the independently produced *Good Pub Guide* and prides itself on its friendly service. The inn is open all day on a Sunday and from noon until 3pm, and from 5pm during the week. Real Ales — perhaps Morlands, Old Speckled Hen, Tetleys and the guest beer, Brakspears — are on offer, and there are quality wines too.

Food is served every lunchtime and evening, and the menu, which changes daily, consists of a wide selection of well-known, favourite dishes, as well as exciting, modern food. All tastes and appetite sizes are catered for, whether you want simply soup, a sandwich or scones, or a main meal with a wicked pudding! Another bonus is that all the food is home-made and the bread is baked locally.

Today *The Windmill* retains its rustic charm and rural character and, in a traditional yet lively atmosphere, provides genuine hospitality — real ales, real food and real service. It's worth a visit!

Walk this way ...

Leave the pub and turn left down the road, passing Ashley Farm, Honeysuckle Cottage and aptly-named Holly Cottage, before turning right down a footpath into a mixed wood of silver birch, oak and beech. Exit from this over a stile at the far side and cross a field, passing three trees on the left — remnants of a former hedge. Drop down to the bridge over a stream and keep ahead again to a stile in the facing fence, then keep to the right along the hedge.

Ignore a right turn as you pass a farm and go through the gap into the next field. Continue beside the hawthorn hedge to a stile, then continue through a rough area and across a stream. From here follow a rough track down the hedge until it bears left at the field's far end and descends to a stream, which runs placidly down a pretty, grassy valley, before ascending to Harrop Green Farm.

A small gate takes you into the farmyard, then turn right down the farm road for a short distance before turning right again over a stile.

Keep the hedge on your right until you leave it at a waymarker and turn left up to a stile. Walk diagonally across the next, huge field, on a grassy track which narrows to a path after a dip and eventually reaches a stile in the corner by woodland — Barton's Clough. Turn right here along the sandy track of the Middlewood Way.

Stretching from Rose Hill (Marple) to Macclesfield, this converted railway line forms a pleasant bridleway, with wheelchair access at several points. The walker's path avoids the cuttings and gives superb views of Bollington, White Nancy and the surrounding countryside.

You soon pass Higher Doles Farm, after which, if you want to curtail the walk, you can turn right over a stile, keep left to Holehouse Lane and turn right again back to *The Windmill.*

However, for the whole walk, keep along the Middlewood Way, passing Lodge Farm, where touring caravans used to occupy a breezy field and pretty pussy willows flank the track as you continue to the former Bollington Station, which has toilets.

Opened in 1869, this had 13 staff in its heyday, when the gentry would travel to London by train from here, taking their horse and carriage with them. Sadly, the line was closed in the Beeching cuts of 1970.

Continue ahead to traverse the 20-arched viaduct high above the River Dean and, after walking under a bridge blackened by the smoke of countless trains, you soon reach Grimshaw Lane. As you cross this busy road you can't miss the massive bulk of the Adelphi Mill.

By 1874 a large goods yard south of Grimshaw Lane served the cotton mills with imported coal from Poynton Colliery and exported gritstone from the nearby Kerridge quarries. And here the Macclesfield Canal runs almost parallel to the abandoned railway.

Continue down the Middlewood Way to Clarke Lane, where the stone bridge is well supported by a brick wall and you leave the Way, turning right past Pool House and Kerridge Cricket Club. Next, turn

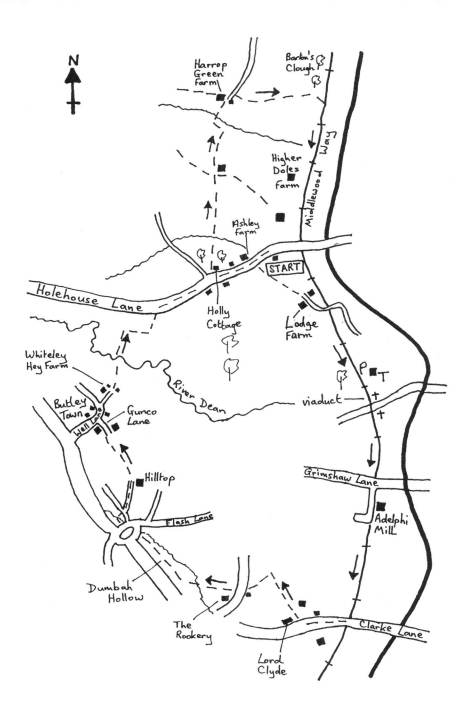

N

Harrop Green Farm

Barton's Clough

Higher Doles Farm

Middlewood Way

Ashley Farm

START

Holehouse Lane

Holly Cottage

Lodge Farm

P T

viaduct

Whiteley Hey Farm

River Dean

Butley Town

Well Lane

Gunco Lane

Grimshaw Lane

Adelphi Mill

Hilltop

Flash Lane

Dumbah Hollow

The Rookery

Lord Clyde

Clarke Lane

right again down a narrow, wall-edged path as you reach a row of terraced cottages, built in 1834 using Kerridge stone. The farthest one is both a listed building and a pub, the *Lord Clyde*, which boasts hand-drawn *Real Ale*.

Cross a stream and continue along a sandy path to a stile and playground, where you turn left by the hedge. You soon reach a house — once the *Drum and Monkey*, now just a number. Cross the busy road here and keep ahead, over a stile and past *The Rookery* before dropping down fields. Electricity sizzles through overhead wires as you keep to the right of a massive pylon and descend to a stream.

Cross this, climb up the bank and turn right, following the stream down Dumbah Hollow all the way to Flash Lane. Cross over and descend down steps to a stile. Keep ahead after this, then turn right over the stream and walk behind a fruit and vegetable stall to a stile. (You may wish to purchase some fruit here to eat along the way.)

Go forward up a tarmac drive, passing the cluster of houses at Hilltop to reach a stile, surrounded by snowdrops or creamy-yellow daffodils in Spring. With the hedge on your left, continue down a grassy track and over stiles to a rough road, peculiarly known as Gunco Lane. At its end, turn right into Well Lane and walk past 18th century cottages, through quaintly named Butley Town.

Turn right up the drive of Whiteley Hey Farm. Continue forward at its end (don't deviate to right or left) through three gates before

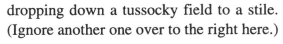

dropping down a tussocky field to a stile. (Ignore another one over to the right here.)

Cross the next field to a turquoise bridge over the River Dean, which you can't miss! Walk up the next field by the hedge and bear right round to a stile onto Holehouse Lane. Turn right along this and walk through Whiteley Green back to *The Windmill*.

AROUND DISLEY

Start: Parking is difficult at *The Ploughboy* so this walk starts in the lay-by along Mudhurst Lane. (SJ 983 832)

Route: Mudhurst Lane - Above Rocks Farm - Seven Springs Camp - Higher Disley - Ring o' Bells Lane - Cockhead - Bollinhurst Reservoir

Distance: 5 miles

By Car: Take the A6 east from Stockport. Pass the entrance to Lyme Park, then turn right up Buxton Old Road in the centre of Disley. Turn right again up Mudhurst Lane on the edge of town and park in the large lay-by on the right.

The Ploughboy
Tel: 01663 766003

Of ancient pedigree, *The Ploughboy*'s history is gradually being pieced together. Once two cottages, then a butcher's shop, stone steps lead down to an ancient well under the stone-flagged floor and the tiny taproom was once the landlord's sitting room. Many of the original, old oak beams are still intact and show the size of the original 'two up, two down' dwelling.

A survey early in the 1850s mentions an alehouse at Danebank Cottages and, as this is the only cottage with both well and cellar, it seems reasonable to assume that locals were congregating to drink beer on the premises as early as that.

Higher up the road A J P Taylor reared his family. Intending but a brief sojourn here before settling in the Lake District, he liked it so much he stayed. *The Ploughboy* is mentioned several times in his autobiography and Dylan Thomas, when a guest of AJP, having drunk the barrel dry at his house, repaired here.

In April 1935 the young Dylan Thomas, aged 21, stayed with the Taylors for a month. He was a difficult and often distasteful guest but AJP made him work for his keep and he painted the outside of his cottage. Later on AJP grew to dislike Thomas intensely and ridiculed his poems.

Today, *The Ploughboy* opens all day at weekends but only from 4pm during the week. However, if asked in advance, the friendly landlord and his wife will be delighted to open up and provide food for a walking group during the day. As an added incentive, this is a *Real Ale* pub, with *Boddies* and Marston's *Pedigree* always available, as well as three keg beers, three lagers, Guinness and Strongbow cider.

Bar food includes home-made soup, rolls and sandwiches, plus daily 'specials' such as lasagne or hotpot, and a barbecue during the summer months, when there's seating outside, both under the verandah and in the back garden.

This is an unspoilt, friendly little pub, with darts, quizzes and karaoke in the evenings and a bookcase where locals exchange books to raise money for St Anne's Hospice. It's definitely worth a visit.

Walk this way ...

From the lay-by turn right and walk up the road to Bolder Hall. Turn left over a stile just past Bolder Hall Farm, with its cattery and craft studio, then walk straight across the field to another stile and follow the insignificant, grassy path up the field ahead, then through reeds to a signpost. Keep ahead again and turn left at a second signpost, before windswept hawthorn bushes.

The views behind open up as you walk uphill. You may need to veer slightly left to cross the ditch and tumbledown wall, before looking for the stile ahead and a path to the top. (Keep the parallel wall far to

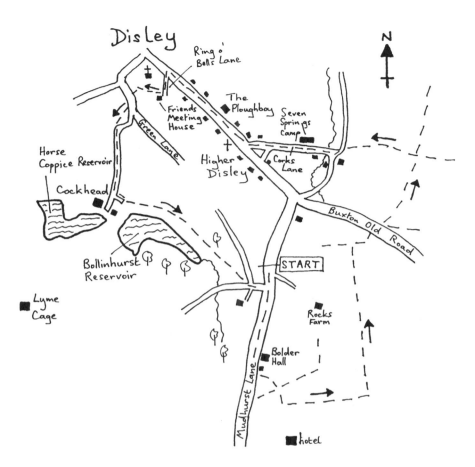

the right.) Turn left along the ridge, following the wall which may give you some protection on a parky day. Cut through a gap part-way along to avoid the crags and notice the wind-eroded boulders — some poised precariously.

After passing the remains of a sheepfold, climb over a step-ladder stile and continue with the wall on your right to a high stile — a heave-up for short legs. The views over to Kinder make this an exhilarating part of the route.

Drop down the next field between gorse bushes, veering left at the bottom, along the wall to a gap at its end into the next field. Then make for a signpost ahead, before the telegraph pole, and turn right. Walk through a small coppice separated by two stiles — the second straddling a horizontal, stone gatepost. Keep in the same direction alongside a wall to two more stiles at a stable, then veer left down the field and climb over the stile onto Buxton Old Road.

Go over the stile opposite, into a field which may be home to a donkey. Ignore the stile to the right as you drop down the field to another stile in the far corner. Keep the barbed-wire fence on your left as you continue down the valley side, then turn left over a stile when you reach a facing wall.

Stay in this direction, beside the wall, until you go over a stile into a spinney of firs, then over a cattle grid. Bear left and right here, to cross the stream, which may be muddy. Continue in this direction (uphill at first) on the track past Seven Springs Camp.

After passing Kinder View look out for the obsolete Victorian postbox in the wall, replaced by a later one as you reach the end of Corks Lane. Turn right past the Methodist chapel to *The Ploughboy*.

Stop for refreshment. *If shut continue to The Mousetrap, or any of the other eating places in Disley.*

Continue downhill and, at the bottom, turn left up Ring o' Bells Lane, by the White Horse Hotel. Pass several 19th century buildings and continue to the Friends Meeting House — once the *Ring o' Bells* inn.

But a stone's throw from Disley's traffic-laden centre stands this 17th century stone building set in the most attractive grounds — a place of peace. Built as an inn, probably by the Legh family of Lyme Hall for their workforce, its licence was rescinded early this century by teetotal Lady Newton, after which it became a home for retired estate workers. The Society of Friends eventually bought the property from the Lyme estate in 1939 for the princely sum of £280.

Since then it has been renovated, most recently by a resident warden, a craftsman carpenter whose trademark, a woodpecker, can be found carved in some of the ancient beams. Relics unearthed on the premises include tiny medicine bottles and coins dug from the garden, smoking pipes, thimbles and a George II groat (worth half a farthing). Now restored, the vertical window above the staircase was bricked in during Victorian times when it was considered improper for ladies to be seen retiring to bed!

Turn right under the sign depicting five bells, cross the stream and bear left, through the gate and up steps, passing the cemetery of Disley Church. At its end turn left through the fence onto a grassy path. Walk up the field, then turn left again, along Green Lane.

Turn right immediately over a stile and cross the field diagonally towards Lyme Cage, which stands out on the hillside far ahead. Climb over the stile behind the gap in the hawthorn hedge and turn right down the road.

On reaching Cockhead turn left at the signpost to Moorside, climb over a stile and walk up the field parallel with both fence and road. Continue alongside the wall, with a view across Bollinhurst Reservoir. Negotiate a stile in a wall then continue in the same direction over marshy ground to a stile after the reservoir's end.

Stay near the wall at first, then walk along a pretty path above a stream to a stile, with dog panel, in a fence. Continue up the field, with a fence and gorse on your left, all the way to a signpost on your right. Exit through the gate here and turn left back up to Mudhurst Lane, where you turn left again to the lay-by and journey's end.

AROUND LAMALOAD RESERVOIR

Start: Carpark, with picnic area and toilets, at the north end of Lamaload Reservoir (SJ 975 753)

Route: Lamaload Reservoir - Ankers Knowl Lane - Eaves Farm (remains) - Andrew's Edge - Shining Tor - Thursbitch - Redmoor Brow - Nab End

Distance: 6.5 miles

By Car: Leave Macclesfield on the A537 towards Buxton. Take the next left turn after passing the *Setter Dog* pub, signposted Saltersford and the Goyt Valley. Turn left into the carpark at the far end of Lamaload Reservoir .

To reach *The Stanley* after the walk, turn right out of the Lamaload carpark. Cross the A537 and keep ahead. Ignore a road from the right, then keep left as the road goes off to Wildboarclough and the pub carpark is on your left.

The Stanley
Tel: 0160 252414

The Stanley has been a country inn since early in the 18th century. Its open fires, fresh food and warm welcome provide a cosy retreat after a wild and windy trek. *The Stanley* is also a Marston's pub and their *Smooth Brew* on tap will invigorate any weary walker.

The Stanley is open all day for food at the weekend and from noon to 2.30pm during the week. On Sundays, a special, reasonably priced, two-course meal has a choice of two roasts. Everything is home-cooked, and their own pies — lamb and mint, meat and potato, steak and kidney — are all popular. There's also a 'specials' board and an *à la carte* menu in the evening.

Walk this way ...

Walk down to the picnic area which overlooks the reservoir and turn right. Follow a track downhill over a stream, then uphill over a stile and along a rough track to a gateway. From here turn left downhill to the waterworks.

Keep left along the wall here, crossing the River Dean, then bearing left in front of a gate. Climb uphill beside a fir plantation, walking towards Ankers Knowl Lane. After a stile, and perhaps a pause to admire the view, continue through a woodland of mostly deciduous trees, including rowan, beech and oak, to stone steps in a wall.

Keep ahead over the next field, walking to the right of a prominent wooden post to reach more steps in a wall. Continue forward beside an electric fence, negotiate a stile by a gate and drop down a stony track beside a wood.

Notice the worn and flattened paving, then a grassy 'green lane' — perhaps an ancient routeway.

After passing a substantial barn, probably used as a lambing shed, go over a stile by a gate. Cross a stream and continue along a stony track beside the wood until another stile leads onto Ankers Knowl Lane.

Turn left downhill to cross the stream gushing down to the reservoir through natural woodland (mainly beech) which provides delightful, dappled shade. Continue between banks of bracken to a view over sheep-strewn fields to the reservoir. The sweet smell of hay may permeate the air from rolls of black polythene and there's another sturdy lambing barn.

The weary or faint-hearted can return along the lane to the carpark.

Unfortunately, the signpost to Burbage via Shining Tor is in a dip, which means a drop downhill only to ascend again! Then turn right over the stile here and walk up a grassy track beside bushes of golden gorse. Ignore a stile to the left and climb up to the one ahead.

The far-reaching views are a delight as you trudge ever higher.

Continue forward up a faint path. (Take it easy up here unless you are a fitness freak or have something to prove!)

Windgather Rocks stand out stark and rugged to the north and Jenkin's Chapel is hidden in trees.

Climb over the next stile and continue uphill, veering right (through reeds at first) then along a fence and between stone posts. Shutlingsloe's pyramidical peak stands out ahead as the path follows the fence round a corner, then stays parallel to it. (It's easy walking if you're not heading into a gale force wind!) Finally, climb over a stile and keep ahead again ready for the last steep pull to the summit.

The communications mast on Croker Hill is clearly visible and the Jodrell Bank telescope stands out on the plain below.

Reaching the ridge, climb over another stile and turn right along a grit path — a vast improvement on the boggy track which used to exist along here. To reach the trig point (S2773), turn right over a step-ladder stile.

You are now standing at the highest point in Cheshire.

It's a boring walk along the ridge to Cats Tor, with no views, so retrace your steps to the stile, then negotiate the knee-knocking descent to the earlier stile below. In front of this turn right long the fence and keep forward over another stile, with only a curlew's call for company.

On reaching a facing wall, dog-leg left through tumbledown stones, then stay in the same direction as before across the next field, on a tiny path but with the wall over to your right. At the wall ahead walk through the green area and continue downhill on a barely visible path until you end up at a sturdy stile with a stream to its left.

After the stile, drop down to the stream and stride over it (a flat stone will help), then bear right up the hillside and alongside another tumbledown wall until, at its end, you go through it and turn left (in front of a rusty gate).

Todd Brook burbles below — a perfect place for a paddle and picnic!

Continue with the wall, then the stream, on the right, to stone steps in the wall ahead. Keep forward again on a tiny path, over a flattened

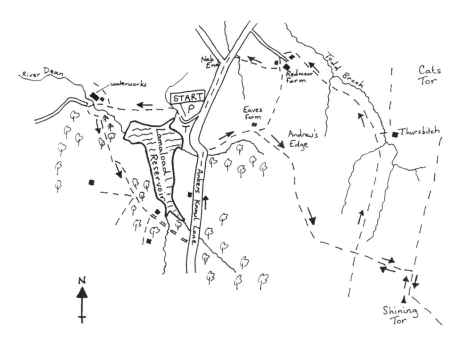

wall and along the hillside until you drop down to leap over a tributary stream and climb up to a sturdy step-ladder stile in the wall ahead.

From here, walk straight uphill, veering right to a post at the corner of two walls. Go through the gap here, then veer right, uphill again, and make for a 'stile' where a wall becomes a fence to the right of Redmoor Farm.

Walk diagonally up and across the next field, behind the farm, to a stile in the far corner, then continue to a stone stile which wobbles! Cross the track here and continue through the farmyard, past a large barn and through a farm gate.

Walk straight down this field to the wall and fence at the bottom, where there's a stile. Keep descending in the same direction, with reeds on your right and a prominent green, white and orange post near a concrete base.

From here, continue to drop down through reeds and open spaces, making for the gate ahead onto the road. Well to its right is a stile over the wall, which you reach after crossing the stream. Turn left along the road, up to Nab End and a view, then keep left towards Wildboarclough and you will soon reach journey's end.

AROUND TEGG'S NOSE

Start: Leather's Smithy (SJ 953 715)

Route: Ridgegate Reservoir - Macclesfield Forest - Walker Barn (Setter Dog) - Gulshaw Hollow - Bull Hill Lane - Tegg's Nose - Bottom's Reservoir

Distance: 6 miles or 4.5 miles

By Car: Leave Macclesfield on the A523 (the Leek Road) and take the first left turn to Langley. Keep ahead through the village, passing Bottoms Reservoir. *Leather's Smithy* is on the left overlooking Ridgegate Reservoir.

Leather's Smithy
Tel: 01260 252313

This attractive inn took its name from the first licensee, William Leather. On the wall outside is a plaque with his initials on it — WCL (William Charles Leather). The date of 1821 is also shown but the building may be older than that.

William Leather was employed by Stancliffe's Brewery to run the pub and be the firm's farrier, shoeing the horses which pulled the draycarts. Both he and his family are buried nearby in St James' churchyard, Sutton, where inscriptions on their tombstones, though weathered, are still legible. The inn sign is an authentic reproduction of a photograph of William Leather, which captures his likeness well.

For a time the pub was called the *New Inn*. The reason for this stemmed from the mid-1800s, before which time ale houses only sold ale (usually home-brewed) and porter. When a new law was passed by parliament allowing licences to be granted for pubs to sell wines and spirits too, many pubs changed their names to the *New Inn*, to show they'd been granted the new licence.

The inn stocks a large variety of traditional beers, including Banks, Marstons and Morrells, together with imported Czech lager on draught from the oldest brewery in Czechosolvakia. The landlord for the last 20 years also prides himself on his large selection of malt whiskies — about 80 in total.

All pockets and tastes in food are catered for — from the popular black pudding and chips to steaks. Most of the food is home-made, including several vegetarian dishes and daily 'specials', and there is an excellent selection of puddings.

The bar boasts its original flagged floor and a small function room, seating 25, is an ideal venue for meetings. In Winter, blazing open fires add to the cosy atmosphere and, in Summer, the pretty garden provides stunning views. Walkers are always welcome.

A further attraction is the pianola. Manufactured by Weber in March 1927, it combines a German mechanism with an English case. It can be played as a piano for a sing-song but, for a real treat, the landlord may be persuaded to perform *Daisy, Daisy* on it!

Walk this way ...

From the carpark turn left past the pub and keep left up the road past Higher Ridgegate Farm. When this road veers right keep ahead up the bridleway, from where you have a clear view over the plain to Jodrell Bank's saucer-shaped telescopes. Take the middle track when you reach a junction along here (signposted to Walker Barn), then continue past a barn towards Tegg's Nose. (The signpost to Walker Barn here takes you via the road.)

The plantations forming Macclesfield Forest were begun as early as 1928 when they were first planted by Macclesfield Water Board. They mainly consist of larch and spruce, which do well on the poor

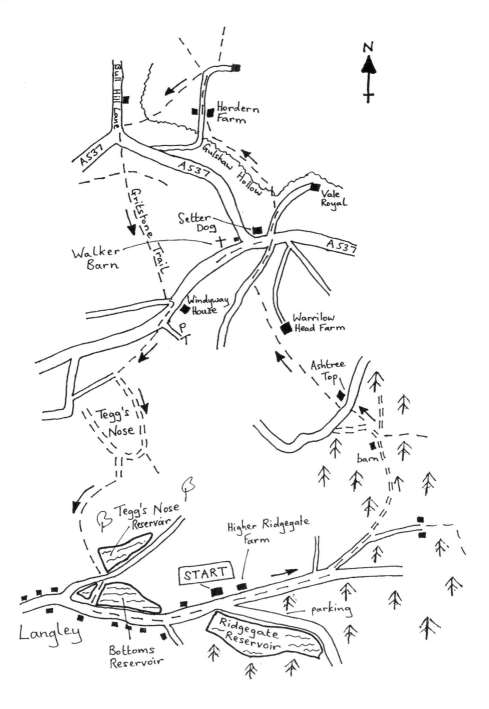

soil, and the last wolf in England is supposed to have been slain while prowling through this forest.

Take the next right turn to Walker Barn, up a tiny path. On reaching a tarmac road turn left, and immediately right up steps and over a stile into a field. With Ashtree Top on your right keep along the side of the field to another stile and take the same direction down the next field.

The views are superb. The telecom tower stands aloft on Croker Hill, known locally as Piggy Big Ears because it's always listening in!

Cross the stream in the valley and keep forward over the hill (alongside a tumbledown wall) into the next valley, then climb the hill to another stile. After passing Warrilowhead Farm go through the gap in the wall and keep ahead over the next field to a step-ladder stile. (You are walking parallel with the road along here.)

Drop diagonally left down the next field to a high step-ladder stile onto the farm road, where you turn right and, in Spring, pass daffodils nodding in the breeze. Turn left at the main road down to the *Setter Dog* — a good place for a refreshment stop.

For the short walk ...
Turn left from the Setter Dog to pass Walker Barn Methodist Church.

This Wesleyan chapel dates from 1863. The tiny community it serves grew up in the middle of the last century, when a toll bar was set up here on the turnpike road into Derbyshire.

As you walk along here Shutlingsloe vies with Tegg's Nose for most prominent landmark and you pass aptly-named Windyway House.

For the long walk ...
Climb over the stile at the side of the *Setter Dog* and continue down the track, soon turning left after a gully, which you follow into Gulshaw Hollow. Cross the stream and stile here, then bear left along a fence, then walls, all the way to the Hordern Farm complex.

Continue ahead, up the track, for splendid views over industrial Hurdsfield, along the Saddle of Kerridge and into Rainow. However, you soon turn left over a stile and join the Gritstone Trail, which you follow for almost all the rest of the walk.

Continue beside the wall to a stile in the corner, cross the next field to a stile by a steel gate, then drop downhill in the dip to cross the stream. Immediately, bear left at the far side of a huge holly bush to reach a stile behind it and continue uphill to a stile by a barn. Then continue over the hill's brow to reach a stile and Bull Hill Lane.

Cross the busy A537 here and make for a stile on your left. (Take great care.) Walk beside the overgrown quarry, then along the wall to a stile in the field's far corner. Continue uphill, following the visible grassy path and passing some breezily perched picnic tables on the way to another stile. Veer right to a step-ladder, then ahead and leftish on flattened grass to a stile, a tumbledown wall and further stiles to reach the road at Windyway House, where you turn right.

To complete both walks ...

At Windy Way carpark it's worth pausing at the viewfinder.

The rock forming this area is millstone grit, an especially hard sandstone which is excellent for building both roads and houses. The whole area is pitted with quarries. Tegg's Nose Quarry closed in 1955, reopening as a country park in 1972. Further on there's a display of old quarrying tools and machinery.

Return to the road and go ahead, following the signpost to Croker Hill through a kissing gate. At more gates, turn left up rough-hewn steps to the Tegg's Nose summit. From another viewfinder you can see Scragg Works, known for its manufacture of textile machinery, then return to the path and keep along it until you turn left over a stile.

The unusual name, Tegg's Nose, may originate from a time when a local Norseman named Tegga owned the land (naze). Alternatively, 'tegg' is an old name for a lamb and it's said that the hill's profile before quarrying resembled a sheep.

Keep following the Gritstone Trail markers, enjoying glorious views over Langley and the reservoirs below until you eventually turn left down steps, then descend rapidly on a wide path between gorse, reeds, heather and bracken to steep steps, a gate and a carpark.

Cross the road here and continue over the bridge and above the overflow channel, then keep ahead beside Bottoms Reservoir before bearing left and eventually cutting through a gap in the wall onto the road. From here turn left uphill. The Gritstone Trail goes off to the right before you reach High Low Farm, and *Leather's Smithy* soon comes into sight.

WEST CHESHIRE
AND WIRRAL

Hockenhull Platts   *Bird in Hand*

Starting in Guilden Sutton, this walk follows part of the Longster Trail to Great Barrow, then crosses the medieval packhorse bridges at Hockenhull Platts.

Hoylake   *Farmers' Arms*

Enjoy a visit to the seaside, walking along the sands to West Kirby, then continue along the Wirral Way and relax in Royden Park after your exertions.

Ness   *The Harp*

Memories of the past are evoked in the relics of Denhall Colliery, a trip along the deep and silent cutting on the Wirral Way is an eerie experience and the Dee's marshland teems with wildlife.

Shocklach   *The Bull*

Follow part of the *Welsh Marches* route and enjoy one of Cheshire's hidden gems in St Edith's Church, Shocklach, with its ancient cross and splendid Norman arch.

Thurstaston   *Cottage Loaf*

Visit Wirral's only waterfall as it plunges down the Dungeon. Watch small birds feeding in the hide at the Thurstaston Centre, then climb onto the common for the breathtaking views over the Dee to Wales.

A Place to Visit

Brimstage Hall

The hall itself, now a private residence, dates back to medieval times, when it was probably much bigger, and its pele tower was a refuge for the local people in those distant, turbulent times. Arrow slits and the machiolated roof still remain. From the latter, boiling liquid could be poured onto attackers, and a clockwise, spiral staircase allowed a retreating defender free use of his sword arm. Faint traces of a moat are still visible in the adjacent fields but the defensive earth embankment has long since disappeared.

Folk come from afar to visit this craft centre, which has grown up around the courtyard of the old hall. It includes one of Britain's finest embroidery centres, a restaurant renowned for home cooking and many other craft workshops. In the 12th century crypt a range of gifts can also be purchased, from pictures and preserves, to greeting cards and local books. (Tel: 0151 342 7558)

About Wirral ...

Wirral has a long and varied history, dating back to Roman times when an outpost of the Chester garrison was established at Meols on the north-west corner. Norse and Celtic influences are also prevalent in both relics and place names.

Today, the Dee estuary is of international importance as a breeding ground for waterfowl and a vital stopping place for migrating birds. It is also noted for other wildlife, such as the natterjack toad.

Since the 1974 boundary changes, the north end of the Wirral peninsular (just north of Neston on the River Dee to Eastham Locks on the River Mersey) has been annexed from Cheshire.

AROUND HOCKENHULL PLATTS

Start: Guilden Sutton parish carpark (SJ 448 680)

Route: Guilden Sutton - Great Barrow - Tarvin - Hockenhull Platts - Cotton Lane - Vicar's Cross

Distance: 7.5 miles

By Car: Take the A51 east from Chester. Pass Vicar's Cross Golf Course, then take the next left turn down Wicker Lane. Turn left in the village of Guilden Sutton down Church Lane — a No Through Road. Other than on a Sunday, if walking first please use the parish carpark on the right. (Adjacent, there's a small, lawned garden for picnics.)

Bird in Hand

Tel: 01244 300341

This old coaching inn was rebuilt in the 1920s when the thatched roof caught fire and, at one time, the stream running under the pub used to flood after heavy rain. Its selection of Real Ales has earned it a place in Camra's Top Twenty Cheshire inns.

The *Bird in Hand* is also renowned for its food, with an extensive menu plus blackboard 'specials', and all the dishes are freshly cooked. The inn also specialises in unusual fish, such as red mullet, bream and parrot fish. Vegetarians are not forgotten, with delectable dishes such as bird's nest fruit and vegetable curry, or baked avocado with Stilton and walnuts, from which to choose.

Food is served every day, at lunchtime and in the evening.

Walk this way ...

Turn left back to the junction, then go right towards Stamford Bridge and Tarvin and almost immediately left past Hill Farm House, Tile Barn and Tile Fields. Keep ahead over a stile, then walk, with the hedge on your left, to another stile at the field's far end. Continue ahead again, on a path between crops, to a stile at the far end and a bridge over a ditch. Turn right alongside this.

*At the field's end you join the **Longster Trail** and follow it all the way to Great Barrow. Ten miles long, this waymarked route runs from the outskirts of Chester to the summit of Helsby Hill. Devised by Frank Longster, one-time chairman and active member of the Mid-Cheshire Footpath Society, sadly he died before the route was complete.*

Climb over a green, metal stile and turn left, crossing concrete bridges over the River Gowy and a tributary, then a stile. Keep ahead across the field, making for a lone tree. Turn right here and walk alongside a deep ditch until you cross a bridge over another ditch, then walk up the side of the next field to exit by a kissing gate beneath an oak. Continue up the side of the next two fields, climb over a stile and bear right along a track, which becomes a country lane.

On the left you pass *Greysfield*, an attractive, half-timbered building. Keep ahead at the crossroads, passing *The White Horse* pub, which serves food and is open all day on a Saturday, then keep ahead again at the village pump, down Mill Lane.

Where the lane ends before Mill House, bear right by a black gate, walking up a track until, near the top, you turn right up sandstone steps and go through a gate into a field. Walk ahead with the hedge on your left and a maze of rabbit holes in the bank beside you!

After crossing a stile and planks over a ditch, turn left alongside the hedge to another stile, then turn right, under wires, with the hedge on your right. Negotiate a criss-cross stile and walk in the same direction down the next, long field. The stile at its end bears the notice, *Please lift and replace* and the top section lifts out of the way for ease of use.

Veer left over the next field, under wires again, to a stile in the far left-hand corner. Cross the ditch here, then continue uphill with the hedge on your left. Turn left over two stiles at the top of the field and continue alongside the right-hand hedge until you climb over a stile by a grey gate.

Continue along a short track and cross the busy A54 with care. Keep ahead down a short road, then briefly turn left down the road into Tarvin, before turning right down Hockenhull Lane. At the far end of this bear left and continue along this lane — now a No Through Road.

Cross the A51 and keep ahead again. At a grassy triangle, where the road winds right to Hockenhull Hall, keep ahead and walk down a track, which follows the hedge down to Platts Lane. Turn right and continue to Hockenhull Platts.

*Known locally as the **Roman Bridges**, these three packhorse bridges with cobbled surface, which span the River Gowy and its tributaries, are, in fact, medieval in origin. Incredibly, this was once the main thoroughfare from London to Chester. However, as the bridges were never wide enough even for carts, by the 18th century other roadways had taken their place. Yet the atmosphere surrounding them is still charged with past history.*

Keep in the same direction until you turn right along Cotton Lane, then turn left over cobbles as you reach Cotton Hall. Keep ahead past barns and byres, then continue in the same direction across a field, beside a hedge and straight over the following field, dropping down to a bridge into the next one.

Veer left over the hilltop in a further field, then drop down to the stile in the facing hedge, near Hollows Farm. From here, cross planks over the ditch and keep ahead up to a stile by a gate. Turn right along the road, passing the end of an old green lane, on the way to the busy A51.

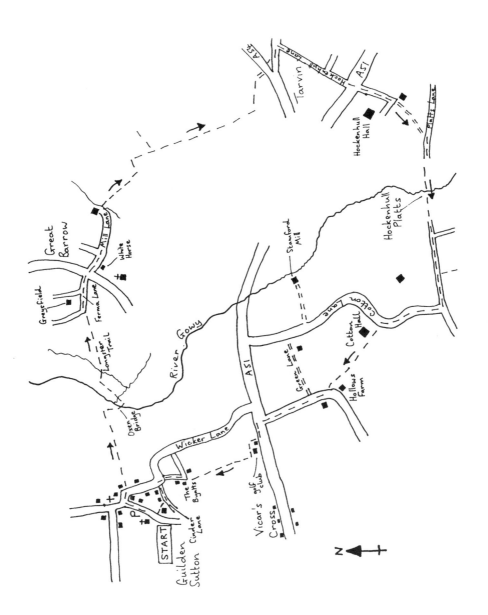

Tarvin

Hockenhull Lane

A51

A51

Platt Lane

Hockenhull Hall

Hockenhull Platts

Great Barrow

Mill Lane

White Horse

Greyfield

Ferma Lane

Stamford Mill

Cotton Lane

Longster Trail

River Gowy

A51

Green Lane

Cotton Hall

Oxen Bridge

Hollows Farm

Wicker Lane

The Byatts

Vicar's golf club

Guilden Sutton

Cinder Lane

Cross

START

N

- 168 -

Cross to the opposite footpath with care and turn left. Turn right at a footpath sign by the first opening in the hedge. Walk along to the end of buildings (part of Vicar's Cross Golf Club) then look for the bright blue posts to your left. Follow these, first in front of the clubhouse, then across the course.

The whole route is clearly waymarked — a credit to the club — and mostly winds its way through a sheltering spinney of trees. Exit by the stile at the far end, then keep ahead over a field with a hedge on your left. Negotiate two stiles, separated by the kitchen garden of *The Byatts*, then keep ahead down a track to Wicker Lane.

Turn left here, then left again down Cinder Lane, where you rejoin the Longster Trail. Where the hedge bordering the footpath ends, veer right down a path, by holly bushes, in Winter bright with berries. This leads down to the *Bird in Hand* — well worth a visit before you turn right back to the parish carpark.

AROUND HOYLAKE

Start: Carpark in Royden Park (SJ 246 858)

Route: Royden Park - Saughall Massie Road - Hoylake Station - Green Lodge Hotel - Hilbre Point - West Kirby - Wirral Way - Caldy - Stapledon Wood - Birch Heyes Farm

Distance: 9 miles

By Car: Take the A540 from Chester towards Hoylake. About one mile after Thurstaston, turn right down Montgomery Hill at a mini-roundabout, signposted Frankby. At the *Farmers Arms* junction turn right to stone gateposts into Royden Park. Continue over speed bumps to the crossroads. The carpark and toilets are on the left.

Farmers' Arms

Tel: 01151 6775129

Open all day every day, the *Farmers' Arms* is a homely, country inn, well suited to walkers. The home-cooked, reasonably priced food is served from noon until 3pm, and usually includes lamb stew, hotpot and chilli, and in Summer you can enjoy oven-baked baguettes in the garden. There are no sweets, so that's good for the diet, and food isn't served in the evenings, except for a pre-booked buffet.

There are six cask ales, one of which is always Whitbread.

Walk this way ...

From the carpark in Royden Park walk back to the crossroads and follow the broad avenue, signposted Montgomery Hill and Frankby Mere, to a gate onto the road. Turn right for a few yards, then go left and immediately right along a bridleway, waymarked to Grange.

Cross the B5139 and keep straight on towards Newton, passing livery stables on the right. Continue down a dirt path between sheds to its end, where you turn left, noticing the yellow waymark on a tree. After a footbridge and stile turn left again into the field, then walk beside the wood to another stile.

Cross the next, huge field diagonally to a stile in the far corner, then stone steps lead onto the road. Turn right, passing China Plate Farm.

Note the coat of arms, the date of 1753 and the initials T I E on the front wall of the farmhouse.

Keep straight on at Saughall Massie Road, signposted Hoylake, to pass Long Rake Farm, then go through an iron gate and along a track for almost a mile. Cross a stile and a wooden bridge over Birket Brook — its name probably an old English version of Bridget. Then continue ahead down the field's side to another stile.

Here, turn left along an old green lane and, where it turns right, keep straight on into a field, over a footbridge and stile. Then keep ahead with the ditch on your left, passing under power lines and continuing until you reach a lane over a second stile and footbridge.

Turn right beside the golf course, walking through a small industrial estate, then turning left along Station Road. After passing the entrance to Hoylake Golf Club at a bend, continue over the level crossing at Hoylake station.

This railway line still provides a frequent commuter service between the Wirral peninsular and Birkenhead.

Keep ahead to a roundabout, then straight on along the Kings Gap.

The Kings Gap was the route down which the Royal escort travelled to board ships, when Hoylake was a port for armies sailing to Ireland.

About Hoylake

In the 10th century, Norse settlers from Ireland set up a small community here and a church dedicated to St Bridget.

*The name, **Hoylake**, however, is little more than a century old, but is derived from the earlier, Hoyle Lake, so called when a great sandbank from Hilbre to Meols created a deep water anchorage for sea-going vessels. This was much used by armies sailing to Ireland, including, in 1690, some 10,000 men, led by William III, who fought and won the Battle of the Boyne — an event all too frequently blamed for the 'Troubles' in Northern Ireland.*

With the silting up of the anchorage, and the growth of Liverpool as a port, Hoylake became first a spa town, then a holiday resort, combined with West Kirkby. Later, with the invention of the motor-car and good rail links, the area became increasingly busy with day trippers, many from Liverpool.

You soon reach the *Green Lodge Hotel* — the half-way point of the walk and well worth a visit.

*The **Green Lodge Hotel** was built over 200 years ago as a shooting lodge for Sir John Stanley, Lord of the Manor. Today, there are two bars, which serve Burtonwood ales and guest beers, an excellent restaurant and it is usually open all day. Walkers are welcome, whether for a drink, soup and sandwiches, steak-and-kidney pie, or any other food on offer.*

From The King's Gap turn left down Stanley Road.

Here, you pass the Royal Liverpool Golf Course, a links course which hosts international events. Attractive houses of many styles face it and, at the far end, the old lighthouse is now a private residence.

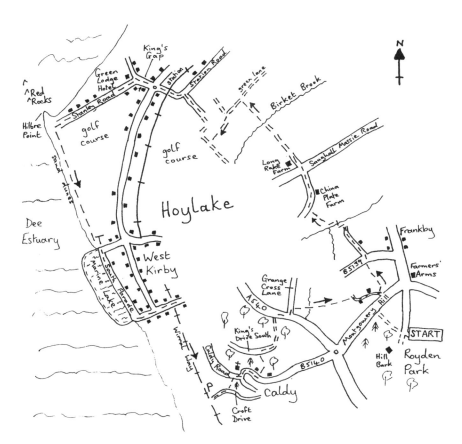

Reaching the beach you may like to turn right to view Red Rocks from Hilbre Point, before turning left along the well-trodden foreshore, with fine views over to the three islands of Hilbre. (In the event of high water a track on the dunes runs along the fence of the golf course.)

At West Kirby, climb the steps and walk along the promenade to the brick building ahead.

Outside are posted the times when it is possible to cross to Hilbre on foot, which takes about an hour, and there are also toilets here.

You may then wish to walk round the outside edge of the lake but don't do so in a high wind unless you are wearing a full set of waterproofs! Otherwise, continue along South Parade.

At the sailing club turn left to the railway bridge, drop down steps at its far side and turn left along the Wirral Way for almost a mile. After passing picnic tables, then a carpark, turn left up Croft Drive. At the right-hand bend turn left again, up a sandy bridleway, to reach the B5140 at Caldy's war memorial.

Turn right down Caldy Road to the crossroads, then wind left uphill on the right-hand footpath. After passing the church, Caldy Wood, a road on the left and the house, *Wood View*, turn left before a white house, up a footpath between stone gateposts.

This delightful path follows traces of an old stone wall on the right and takes you to King's Drive South. Turn right to its end, then continue ahead along a bridleway (ignoring other paths to right and left) to reach the A540 down King's Drive North.

Cross over and turn right, then take the second left turn down Grange Cross Lane. Almost immediately turn right down a narrow path to a footbridge. Cross the field diagonally to reach the far hedge, then walk along it to stone steps onto a lane. This meanders along to the road — Montgomery Hill. Turn right, then left at a wooden gate, waymarked Thurstaston, and retrace your steps.

Royden Park and Hill Bark

Royden Park has been a public, open space since 1961. Once farmland, in the 19th century it was turned into a country estate, much of which can still be seen today, including the walled garden and the Victorian coach-house.

Hill Bark, a half-timbered, mock Tudor mansion, with massive chimneypots, was built on Bidston Hill in 1891 for the wealthy soap manufacturer, R W Hudson. In 1931, it was moved, brick by brick, to its present position. Its interior has magnificent oak panelling and stained glass windows, and the building's surrounded by exotic trees and close-cut wildflower meadows, attractive to butterflies.

AROUND NESS

Start: The Harp (SJ 290 760)

Route: Quayside - Well Lane - Cumbers Lane - Wirral Way - Neston - Old Quay

Distance: 5 miles

By Car: Take the A540 west from Chester. After turns to Puddington and Burton, go left at the next traffic lights — signposted Ness. Drive down to the end of Mill Lane and turn right into Neston Road, which becomes Burton Road. Stay on this until you turn left into Marshlands Road at a mini-roundabout and drive down to the marshes. Either park here, or, if you are patronising *The Harp*, turn left along the rough road (Quayside) to it.

The Harp

Tel: 0151 336 6980

The property dates back to 1711 when it was three cottages. In 1870 two of these were turned into a pub for the miners and it was the Welsh pitmen, with music in their souls, who named it. It is still very much a locals' pub (always a worthy recommendation) and its unspoilt, traditional interior also attracts visitors from all over the world.

Since taking over the pub, Ray and June Oldfield have refurbished the interior but kept the original, tiny rooms intact, the ceilings still crossed by blackened beams, the floors flagged and the walls enhanced by photographs and mementoes from a long-gone mining heyday, including a copy of an original painting of the area from the 1870s. Maroon leather banquettes, padded and buttoned, provide comfortable seats along the walls, further enhancing the atmosphere of this authentic, British hostelry.

The pub is open all day, every day, but, except on Sundays, only serves food at lunchtime (from noon until 3pm) and early evening (5.30 to 7.30pm). The food is traditional and home-made. Puddings are displayed on the blackboard and vary from day to day. In Summer fresh fluke from local rivers is often available, as well as wild Dee salmon and locally-caught shrimps. Sandwiches and huge baguettes are particularly popular with hungry walkers on warm days and, in Winter, there's freshly-cooked hotpot and the comfort of coal fires.

At one time *The Harp* was one of only two beer houses in the area, the other being the *Durham Ox* — now defunct — and today there's enough Real Ale to satisfy any thirsty traveller. Timothy Taylor's *Landlord* and Trophy's *Cask* are always on tap and two other guest beers are changed weekly. Walkers are always welcome. *The Harp* gives a special rate for group bookings but cannot accommodate more than twenty.

The sheltered garden has a play area for children, who are not allowed inside because of licensing laws. Tables on both patio and lawn overlook the silted shoreline and, although *The Harp* is still liable to occasional flooding, at one time the Dee came right to its door.

Walk this way ...

From the pub, turn left and walk alongside the marshes, passing a grassy sward, sheltered by trees — a pleasant place to sit.

Tumbling down from here are massive sandstone slabs, which once formed the wall of Denhall Quay, and now end abruptly where an insignificant runnel gently meanders along — an apology for the once mighty Dee.

As the houses end turn left alongside a fence and continue up a narrow footpath, then a tarmac path bordering the countryside.

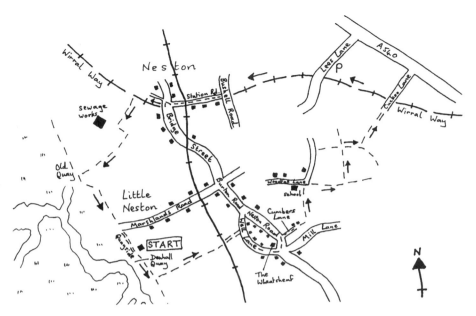

Hedgerows of hawthorn, bramble and elder fringe the fields and, in late Summer, the magenta blooms and huge red hips of rambling roses mingle with lilac-flowering mallow and red-berried cotoneaster.

After negotiating a low stile, continue along a rougher footpath, which becomes a cart-track as you walk under the Chester to Wallasey railway line on the way to Well Lane.

Turn right here alongside huge, sandstone garden walls and enjoy views over the Dee to Wales as you walk along. At *The Wheatsheaf* pub turn left onto Neston Road and walk along the footpath for a short way before turning right down Cumbers Lane. At its end keep ahead on a narrow footpath, passing Cumbers Cottages.

Bear slightly right along the field's edge, then left diagonally across the grass on a tiny path. Make for a stile, behind which is a bright yellow frame supporting swings. Continue between playground and school playing fields to Woodfall Lane.

Here, turn right down a sheltered footpath and take the next left turn along a path, hemmed in by banks topped with bracken, oak and delicious, autumn-fruiting brambles which, after Michaelmas Day, are supposed to be cursed by the devil!

Go through a narrow fence gap and turn right where paths cross. Bear left before a grey, steel kissing gate and keep ahead when the path widens into a cart-track. Turn left just before a bridge, climbing up the embankment to turn left again, along the Wirral Way.

This once busy rail link, stretching for twelve miles between Hooton and West Kirby, was closed in 1962, then opened as Britain's first country park in 1973. The once bustling stations now provide parking and picnic spots along this green, linear route.

Continue under the ornate brickwork of Lees Lane Bridge and enter the sheer-sided cutting, where moss and lichen flourish on the damp walls and small birds, including the tiny wren, nest in crevices.

A train on the local line nearby echoes eerily as you trek silently beside the sandstone walls, reinforced at their base by brick. The line here was dynamited through solid rock and indentations made by pickaxes still pockmark the surface. The squat, triangular 'chimneys' are inspection chambers for a sewer, installed since the railway's demise, its pipe encased in concrete.

At the end of this section of the converted line, cross the main road and keep ahead down Station Road (signposted Wirral Way). Walk under the railway bridge, then cross over and turn left down busy Bridge Street for a few yards. In front of the dismantled bridge climb up steps on the right and continue along the Wirral Way to the next path, waymarked to the Old Quay.

Turn left here and walk down the field's side, across the next field and through a steel kissing gate. Next, go left along a path, then right over another field to a gap in the hedge ahead. Cross the stream and continue to the far end of the following field, where an old, iron kissing gate is hidden in the corner. Finally, walk beside the hedge down the path to the Old Quay.

This is a wonderful spot to pause, rest awhile and imagine the once-bustling quayside. Originally called New Quay, it dates back to 1545, when fishermen unloaded catches of shrimps, crabs and lobsters into donkey-drawn carts. Smugglers too dropped off illegal assignments of spirits, tobacco and tea, and Lord Nelson is reputed to have landed at this wharf on his clandestine visits to Lady Hamilton.

Turn left back to *The Harp*, climbing over a stile of weathered sandstone steps and enjoying extensive views over to the Welsh hills.

Now owned by the RSPB, this marshland is home to the natterjack toad, to sundry bog-loving plants, to kestrels, sparrowhawks and short-eared owls, plus many other birds.

Soon the rushes rustling in the breeze give way to slag heaps and runnels, their blackened slopes partly obliterated by gorse and broom. Further on, the old colliery offices of the local mine are now a private dwelling.

Denhall Colliery was opened here in 1760 by Sir John Stanley of Hooton Hall. However, it proved a difficult mine to work and only produced poor-grade coal, much of which was exported to Ireland and North Wales.

Tunnels were excavated under the estuary for more than a mile, and coal was transported along two subterranean canals to the shafts. Four, narrow, flat-bottomed barges were roped together to form a train, which the miners propelled by lying on the coal and pushing with their feet against the roof.

Many miners originated from Lancashire, Staffordshire and North Wales, and the old terraces of Seven Row and New Street, behind the pub, housed the colliers and their families. Few other relics remain, but road names such as Colliery Green evoke memories of that bustling, bygone time, as also does a visit to The Harp.

AROUND SHOCKLACH

Start: The Bull (SJ 439 492)

Route: Green Lane - Castletown - Grafton Hall - Tilston - Horton Green - Shocklach

Distance: 6.5 miles

By Car: Take the B5130 south from Chester. Cross the A534 at Farndon and continue south to the tiny hamlet of Shocklach. *The Bull* is on the left.

The Bull

Tel: 01829 250239

Locals maintain that *The Bull* has been here for at least 150 years. Today it is certainly thriving. Always popular with locals, its entry in the *Which Good Food Guide* has brought visitors from further afield. All the food is home-made and there's plenty of choice for vegetarians. Parties can easily be catered for, just ring in advance. Food is served from noon to 2pm every day except Monday, and every evening.

To drink, there's Burtonwood beer, both smooth and draught, as well as draught Bass. Also on draught, there's Carling and Labatts lager, Woodpecker and Strongbow cider, and Guinness. There's also a choice of wine.

Walk this way ...

Walk down Green Lane, directly opposite the pub, passing the village school, then White House Farm on the bend. After a stile on the left turn right over the next stile onto the *Marches Way* and cross the field ahead to a stile, keeping to the left of three massive oaks.

*The **Welsh Marches** is an old-fashioned but very apt description of the border between England and Wales, which was continuously fought over from the 13th to the 16th century. The fighting was particularly ferocious in this northern section, between Wrexham and Chester, and the name 'Marches' means disputed territory and boundaries — clearly the case here. Today's **Marches Way** is a long distance walk from Chester to Cardiff.*

Keep ahead across the next field, with extensive views across to Wrexham and the Welsh foothills beyond. Negotiate another stile and plank, then keep ahead again, this time following the left-hand hedge to a stile in the far corner.

Notice the pond teeming with wildlife in the next field — once possibly a marlpit.

Again, continue ahead over this field, eventually walking alongside the hedge to a stile. After this, keep in the same direction to another stile before a small brick building — the old stable.

*The **old stable** was renovated by local people in the Spring of 1993. Under the present brick floor a much older, cobbled surface was discovered, a continuation of which can be seen outside the stable door. 1700 is the date carved into the beam above this and older locals remember the building being used to stable horses while their owners were in church. The remains of stall partitions, harness pegs, tethering rings, a manger and hayracks, together with a hayloft above, were also found.*

Locals also refer to the building as 'the old school' and, although there is no record of this, the room on the first floor appears once to have been snug and warm, with plastered walls and a fireplace. Was it also a dwelling at one time? We may never know.

Continue to the church.

St Edith's Church, *Shocklach, is one of Cheshire's hidden gems. Possibly built by Thomas de Shocklach, whose castle we shall pass later, its oldest part, the nave, dates from about 1150, although its foundations may have been older as its dedication is to St Edith, an Anglo-Saxon abbess.*

The Norman doorway, enriched with its ornately carved, semi-circular arch, is particularly impressive. The ancient cross opposite may have been a meeting place for hiring labourers, buying and selling goods, and passing on local news. The double bellcote, which dates from 1815, houses two bells.

Inside, a stained glass window depicts St Edith, some pews date back to 1697 and the 15th century font is heptagonal. Another delight is the table of commandments in the chancel — purchased for two guineas in 1738.

There was once a musician's gallery and a well-liked curate wrote in the church records, 'I have given the singers a sovereign to preserve peace and harmony'! Another curate comments that some of the villagers may not have attended church because they were too poor to appear 'decently apparelled'.

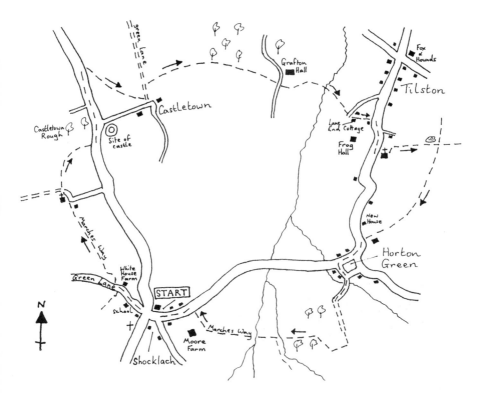

As there are numerous paths and tracks leading to it the church probably once served several communities. Today, the churchyard and adjacent hay meadows are a Site of Biological Importance (SBI).

Leave the church and keep ahead along the cart-track, turning right over a stile round the corner, where you leave the *Marches Way*. Walk straight across two fields and, in the third, start off ahead towards Castletown Rough, then turn sharp right to a stile in the top hedge. Turn left along the road here.

The site of the castle, which gave the area its name, can been seen on the right just before the private road to Castletown House Farm. Along the River Dee there are the remains of castles (or motte and bailey defences) at Aldford, Holt and here near Shocklach, built to deter Welsh invaders. Even earlier, the Romans constructed Deva (Chester) as their bastion against the troublesome tribesmen of North Wales.

Stay on the road until it bears right and you turn right at a waymark, through a double wooden gate. Bear right diagonally across this field, making for farm buildings until you spot a stile in the fence. From here continue diagonally left to a stile beside a steel gate.

You may pass two placid pools, home to a pair of stately swans and many mallard ducks.

Bear right over the next field to a stile near the far corner, after which you jump over the ditch and turn left along a green lane.

This byway to Wetreins Lane, 1.5 miles from here, was used as a road for centuries past — by ox carts, herds of cattle on their way to market and the rich travelling by carriage.

You soon turn right over a stile in the hedge and walk straight down the field, beside a double line of trees, to a stile by a gate. Keep ahead beside the hedge all the way down the next field to the wood. From here leap over the ditch and bear right through the smallish, wooden gate, then continue in the same direction, alongside the wood, to exit the field by another wooden gate.

Walk across the facing field, bearing slightly right and cutting through the line of trees (once part of a hedge). Negotiate two, well-built stiles in the electric fence to reach another in the hedge, then cross a track and another stile.

The sandstone tower of Tilston Church is visible ahead — a typical feature of Cheshire churches. You are also about to pass Grafton Hall, with its huge chimneys.

Bear diagonally left as you drop down the next field to a stile in the fence, then continue downhill, under pylons, to a stile and a concrete bridge over a brook. Walk up the following field, with the hedge on your right, all the way to a stile.

Walk ahead down the drive of Lane End Cottage, then up the lawn to a stile, and keep ahead, following the hedge to another stile onto the road. For a refreshment stop turn left to the *Fox and Hounds* in Tilston, which is open all day. Otherwise, turn right to the church.

St Mary's Church dates from the 14th century when it was the centre of village life. The custom of rush bearing still continues and there's an annual ox roast. Note the plaque on the wall near the gate, in memory of the donor of the double ramp to give access to the raised church door. Notice too the ball-topped pillars, carved with the date 1687, and a skull and crossbones to denote its function as a lychgate, although there is no canopy, or bench on which to rest a coffin.

Turn left to walk through the graveyard, keeping to the left of the church and exiting via mossy, rough-hewn steps and a wooden kissing gate — a tight squeeze for a rotund person wearing a rucksack! Bear left to cross the stream on a stone slab before veering right beside the left-hand hedge. At its corner, continue ahead to a stile by a steel gate at the field's far end.

To the left rises the tree-clad, aptly-named Round Hill at Higher Carden. Farther off are the sandstone hills of Broxton and Bickerton.

Keep ahead with the hedge on your left until you pass a pond before a stile. **Do not climb over this** but turn right, walking down the field to a stile at the far end. Keep ahead down the next field, with the hedge on your left, to a stile in the facing, hawthorn hedge.

Keep ahead again across the next field, with a line of trees on your right, until you reach a hedge corner. Next, continue in the same direction, with this hedge on your right, until you leave it to reach an almost hidden stile at an angle in the facing fence. From here, keep ahead to drop down beside a house to the road.

Turn left and walk down to Horton Green. Take the second left turn (at the village green) to pass Horton Grange — built by H G in 1629. After passing *The Willows* turn right along a track, which you stay on, after negotiating a steel kissing gate, until you turn left down another green lane.

Go through the gate at the end of this and keep ahead, with the hedge on your left. **Do not** climb over the stile into the next field but turn right as you reach it and continue with the hedge on your left until, at a corner, you veer right across to a stile in the facing hedge.

Keep ahead over the following field until you spot a plank bridge and stile in the left-hand hedge, where the wood ends. Negotiate these and walk down beside the wood for a short distance, before veering over to a stile in the hedge at the field's far end.

Continue ahead, beside a sparse hedge, which you must walk through at some point to reach the crossing over a deep ditch. Continue to a wooden bridge between gates, which takes you over a second dyke. (You are now back on the *Marches Way*.)

Keep ahead, with both fence and hedge on your right, to a stile, then walk along a wide, grassy strip beside a field, which may be planted, until it ends and you turn right over a stile by a steel gate. From here keep ahead, with the hedge on your right, to a stile, then turn left along the road back to.the *Bull Inn* and welcome refreshment.

The name, **Shocklach**, *dates from the Norman period and translates as 'a boggy stream, haunted by evil spirits' — presumably a reference to the nearby River Dee.*

Local lore has it that the whole village was moved here, away from the church, at the time of the plague, to get away from the bodies awaiting burial in the churchyard.

AROUND THURSTASTON

Start: Thurstaston Hill (SJ 246 845)

Route: Station Road - The Dungeon - Wirral Way - Thurstaston
Visitors Centre - Links Bridge - Croft Drive East -
Thurstaston Common

Distance: 5.5 miles

By Car: Take the A540 from Chester onto the Wirral peninsular.
Continue through Heswall and, after passing the *Cottage
Loaf* inn, turn right into the Thurstaston Hill carpark.

The Cottage Loaf

Tel: 0151 6482837

Water is a good drink if taken in the right spirit.

What butter and whisky will not cure there's no cure for.

No strangers here, only friends you've yet to meet.

These, and many more quirky quotations can be found on the walls
of this welcoming and attractive pub.

Another wall bears a charter drawn up in 1292 by Thomas, Abbot of Chester and William, son of Patrick of Heswall. It includes a description of the building's site on a hill then called Knukyn. There was also a well, Londymere, walled round with stones, and being on the edge of the manors of Thurstaston and Irby, the residents of both were allowed to use its water freely. Nearby, there was also a house for lepers.

Much later, in the 1920s, the building became a tea-room, then was converted into a pub in the 1950s. Today, it's owned by Whitbread and Real Ales abound. Walkers are always welcome and there are tables outside in Summer. The premises are open all day and food is served between noon and 2pm, and 6 and 9pm on weekdays, and all day at weekends. The menu is diverse, the food reasonably priced and attractive 'specials' are also on offer.

Walk this way ...

From the carpark on Thurstaston Hill, turn left and follow the woodland path, which eventually joins the road. Continue along this to the *Cottage Loaf*. Cross with care here, turn right down Station Road, then left past the parish church of St Bartholomew.

Of the two previous churches on this site, nothing remains of the first, Norman building. However, stone from the second (demolished in the 19th century) was used to built the churchyard wall, and its the tower still stands intact near the present church.

Gothic in style, and with three distinct areas (nave, chancel and sanctuary), the present building seems to have been used by the architect as a practice for his greatest work — Truro Cathedral. Gems inside include a fine, alabaster reredos representing the Resurrection, some richly coloured, stained glass and a font of Mexican onyx with pillars of Blue John stone. In fact, the whole building does have the elegant charm of a mini-cathedral.

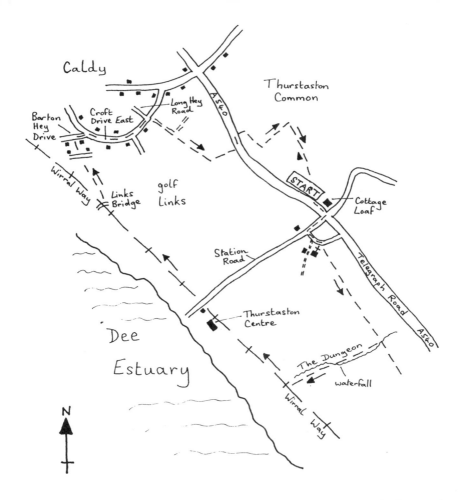

Caldy

Thurstaston Common

Barton Hey Drive

Croft Drive East

Long Hey Road

Ash⊖

Wirral Way

Links Bridge

golf Links

START

Cottage Loaf

Station Road

Telegraph Road

Ash⊖

Dee

Estuary

Thurstaston Centre

The Dungeon

waterfall

Wirral Way

N

Where the road bends left keep straight on down the public footpath towards Heswall, enjoying extensive views over the Dee estuary to Wales. Pass fields, a fir plantation, a stile, a plaque to Arthur Moulson (the open spaces inspector for these parts from 1984 to '96) and a reedy pond.

Then, after another stile, turn right at a waymark to the *Wirral Way* and drop down into The Dungeon alongside a stream. Much of this well-walked path is flagged or boarded, to ease one's passage across tributary streams and the wettest areas. Pass high above the waterfall, then turn left down easy steps into the valley.

The Dungeon has the only waterfall to be found on the Wirral Peninsula. Double back from here to see it and an impressive cave.

Eventually you reach the *Wirral Way*. Either walk down to the beach here and turn right, or turn right under a substantial brick bridge and walk along the *Way*. Both routes lead to the Thurstaston Centre.

At the Centre there are toilets, limited refreshments, much information and a bird hide.

After your visit, continue along the *Wirral Way* until you leave it at the huge, blackened brick structure of Links Bridge. Veer left along a path through a housing development, crossing one road, then turning left at another to reach Barton Hey Drive, where you turn right. At its end turn right along Croft Drive East.

Eventually, bear right down the public footpath to Thurstaston Hill (opposite Long Hey Road) and, where the track bears left, go ahead over a stile, keeping the barbed wire fence on your right. At the end of the field notice the stone with J H 1864 on it before passing through an iron kissing gate and turning left along the hedge.

You soon emerge onto the A540 and turn left to a bus-stop. Cross over here, cut through the wall and turn right along a footpath to Thurstaston Common. Bear left uphill, between gorse bushes, then keep ahead all the way through a belt of silver birch.

There are many paths up onto the hill from here. I veered right for a short way on the path below the hill, then turned left, climbing up a dry stream bed onto the ridge. Turn right along the top, enjoying the view as you walk to the Andrew Blair memorial, then on to the highest point. At the ridge's end, bear slightly right down through the gorse to the carpark.

About the Author

Since moving to Cheshire 32 years ago, Jen Darling has revelled in finding out about the countryside, the wildlife and hidden gems of her adopted county. Always fascinated by both local and natural history, she readily shares with her readers all the knowledge uncovered by her research — whether fact or fantasy.

Married, with four adult children, she was a primary school teacher until 1986, since when she has concentrated on writing and producing outdoor books, together with some local history titles. Her first efforts, *West Cheshire Walks* and *Best Pub Walks in Cheshire* have continued to sell well for *Sigma*, a new edition of the latter having just been produced by them. Other titles, published under her own *Alfresco* imprint, the company she founded in 1991, are listed on the next page.

Jen is a life member of the Mid-Cheshire Footpath Society, plays tennis for a local club and bellrings at her parish church. She is also one of the editors of Warrington's *Talking Newspaper for the Blind* and enjoys gardening, mostly amicably, with her husband!

Although still visiting Cheshire frequently to see family and friends, or to sell books, in 2004 Jen moved back to her native county of Yorkshire, where she hopes to continue to write about rambling around the countryside.

Alfresco Books

Walks in North Cheshire *by Jen Darling*   **Price £**
The only walking book covering the north of the county.   4.95

Orchards of Cheshire, *for Cheshire WI*
A unique book to promote fruit growing.   5.95

Organic Gardening *by Ruth Jacobs*
How to garden in an environmentally friendly way.   3.95

Gardening for Wildlife *by George Pilkington*
Give nature a helping hand. (In the RSPB catalogue)   4.95

The Roof of Africa on Wheels *by Jon Amos*
... follows his ascent of Kilimanjaro in a wheelchair.
(Donation from each sale to physically adapted sport.)   8.95

A Cat in My Lap *by Jenny Melmoth*
... for cat lovers everywhere — written with affection.   8.95

Crosswords for Children — Book One and Book Two
Useful on holiday, wet days, car and plane journeys ...   *each* .95

A Perfect Present

Edwardian Rambles was written early in the 1900s by Henry Josiah Atty, a Warrington printer who, in his free time, cycled around Cheshire, Chester and Wirral, then wrote about and  illustrated his rides. His talent would have gone unnoticed if this manuscript had not been discovered in a wardrobe. Each page is individually illustrated and handwritten.

Edwardian Rambles makes a very special present, perhaps to celebrate a wedding anniversary or a birthday. Available from bookshops for £14.95, or direct from *Alfresco Books*. (Tel: 01729 830868)